INDIA AND MAHATMA GANDHI

INDIA AND MAHATMA GANDHI

RAVINDRA KUMAR

KALPAZ

India and Mahatma Gandhi

Rs. 450

ISBN: 978-81-7835-822-2

Published in 2010 in India by
Kalpaz Publications
C-30, Satyavati Nagar, New Delhi-110052
Ph: 9212729499
E Mail: Kalpaz@hotmail.com

Laser type setting by: Dinesh Kumar
Printing: Gian Ridhi Offset Printers, Delhi

Contents

Foreword

Dr. Ravindra Kumar is one of the few Indian scholars known throughout the Kingdom of Thailand for his deep studies and clarity of thoughts. He is particularly eminent in Thailand as an Indologist and Gandhian scholar. I myself have had some occasions to both listen to his speeches as well as read some of his writings and what has impressed me the most are his way of analysis and expression.

Dr. Ravindra Kumar has visited several universities of Thailand. Besides speaking on various topics related to current affairs he has delivered special lectures on the fundamentals of Gandhism. Many among Thai professors and students have learnt a lot about Gandhi from his lectures.

Mahatma Gandhi's life and his views regarding non-violence are important not just to India and Thailand, but the entire world. Hence, Dr. Ravindra Kumar's following statement seems to be true:

"Even after more than sixty years of his passing away when the world has changed in different manners, almost all spheres of human life have turned over, and due to unprecedented development a new world has emerged, Mahatma Gandhi's ideas seem to be relevant; they call upon the anxious world to resolve newly created complicated problems in these days of unprecedented and suicidal progress and thus to lead the world on the pathway to peace."

In the increasing tempo of development, competition is also increasing at all levels and all in walks of life. In such situation Gandhi's views seem to be relevant for conflict transformation. In Gandhi's way no one is left defeated. All parties reach a win-win situation. Hence, his way is unique, useful and for the welfare of all.

This book is a collection of seven lectures about Gandhi's life and his ideology, delivered in 2007-08 by Dr. Ravindra Kumar at some of the most prestigious universities of Thailand including the University of Siam in Bangkok. Through these lectures he has made known Gandhi's views on important subjects like non-violence, democracy, nationalism, culture and globalization. He has rendered a praiseworthy service to discuss the importance of Gandhi in the global context and India's contribution to world peace.

I believe through this publication people of India, Thailand, Europe and the rest of the world will benefit, particularly those who consider Gandhi's ideas to be relevant for progress and peace in the world. Those who desire resolution of conflicts through peaceful means will also gain from this work.

I welcome this timely work by Dr. Ravindra Kumar, congratulate him and wish him success in his endeavours.

Dhonburi **A. Vachiravarakarn, President**
Thailand **Dhonburi Rajabhat University**

Introduction

During the last fourteen years, i.e. between 1995 and 2009, I have been invited by twenty-one institutions of higher studies and universities of Thailand as a visiting professor and scholar to speak on different social and political issues as well as philosophy, religion, education, culture and civilization. The most amazing and surprising thing I felt during these visits was a keen interest and curiosity of Thai teachers and students towards Mahatma Gandhi's personality and his philosophy. This is why; I spoke at least on one of the aspects of life and works of the Mahatma at the most of the visited institutions and universities. Perhaps a great Indian loved and the most respected by the Thais after Gautama Buddha is none other but Mahatma Gandhi.

On the basis of his works and views Mahatma Gandhi has greatly impressed the people of Thailand. It is but natural for two chief reasons:

Most of the Thais are followers of Buddhism. Buddhism emphasizes upon acceptance of the inevitable Law of Change in human practices. Thai people have in one way or the other accepted this Law in their lives. This is evident from their day-to-day practices and progress they have made at all levels, local and national. Mahatma Gandhi's non-violence-based ideas are also in agreement to this Law of Change. These ideas also categorically stress on the application of the theory as per the demand of time and space. Hence, Thais simultaneously appreciate and respect them.

Furthermore, Gandhi's healthy views on democracy, his stress upon sound public opinion and call for action to establish justice in people's government are generally popular among the Thais. This popularity can be observed particularly in elites and the teaching-community of Thailand. In this regard I would like to mention an episode that occurred in 2007. That year I was invited by the Siam University of Bangkok to speak on Mahatma Gandhi. In those days Thailand was going through a period of serious political instability. Through a revolt Thaksin Sinavatra, the Thai Prime Minister, was removed from his office.

Soon after my speech a professor, quoting a portion of Mahatma Gandhi's Delhi Diary*, asked me a question regarding his views on democracy and mobocracy. In his question he specifically asked whether in India, which is the largest democracy in the world and where democracy is deep rooted, mobocracy ever dominated

* In which Mahatma Gandhi had said, ***"People in democracy should be satisfied with drawing the Government's attention to mistakes, if any. They could remove the Government if they wished to. But they should not obstruct them by agitating against them. Ours is not a foreign Government having a mighty army and navy to support them. They have to derive their strength from the people."***

over the democracy. Another gentleman asked me a question of similar nature, desiring my explanation of what Mahatma Gandhi suggested about strengthening democracy so that it was not converted into a mobocracy.

Both questions were important, and my response to them was clear. What I said in reply is not a matter of much relevance here; a short article based on my answers to them is included in part seven of this work. However, the important and significant point is that the Thais had a great interest in Mahatma Gandhi's views pertaining to democracy. They were impressed by them.

Secondly, for centuries Indian culture has left its deep impression upon the people of Thailand. Centuries before Buddhism reached Thailand the Thais were greatly influenced by the *Vedic*-Hindu way of life, Indian traditions and values. This influence was the main reason that Buddhism became an indivisible part of the life of the people of Thailand soon after its arrival to Siam.

The roots of Buddhism or Buddhist teachings can be found in Indian traditions; they themselves were the revealer of Indian cultural heritage. In the same manner Gandhi's views are rooted in Indian philosophy, traditions and values. Like Buddhist philosophy, Gandhian philosophy calls upon people in a simple, feasible and adaptable manner; therefore, they are loved, liked and admired by the people of Thailand. Thais consider them to be connected to their own culture and therefore express desire to learn and understand them minutely.

This manuscript includes my seven lectures delivered between 2007 and 2009 in six known universities of Thailand on Mahatma Gandhi and his views about India's role and contributions in the world affairs. Those six universities are: Udan Thani Rajabhat University, Suan Dusit Rajabhat University and Siam University, Bangkok, Naresuan University, Phitsanulok, Khon Kaen University, and Dhonburi Rajabhat University.

I believe, this work will provide some interesting information to those who are interested in Gandhism, India and the Indian Way. The younger generation will be able to examine the significance of Gandhi's ideas in current perspectives and India's role in these days of constantly increasing globalization. Moreover, having Gandhism and the welfaristic Indian Way in the centre, they will come forward to accord a right direction to this international process.

I convey my thanks to Ms. Shirley "Sunny" Guiron and Dr. Ram Sharma for their support in reading this manuscript before sending to press.

Meerut [India] **Ravindra Kumar**
15th February 2009

Abbreviations

A. D.	:	After the death of Christ
A. I. C. C.	:	All India Congress Committee
A. I. S. A.	:	All India Spinners' Association
A. I. V. I. A.	:	All India Village Industries Association
B. C.	:	Before Christ
I. G. N. C. A.	:	Indira Gandhi National Centre for Arts

1

India, Hindu-View, Tolerance and Gandhi

"Not being an exclusive religion it enables the followers of that faith not merely to respect all the other religions, but it also enables them to admire and assimilate whatever may be good in other faiths."

-MK Gandhi

Introduction

A section of scientists dealing with human affairs believes that the emergence of man on earth occurred approximately one million years ago. This particular section of scientists has divided the process of evolution of man in different ages: Primitive-Age, Stone-Age[1], Bronze-Age, Iron-Age and Modern-Age. A section of archaeologists has also accepted the arguments of the above scientists dealing with the human affairs particularly in context of their division of ages of evolution. Undoubtedly, this section of archaeologists has its own arguments in this context and the basis of their evidences is the human-instruments found during digging works undertaken from time-to-time.

The argument of scientists dealing with human affairs in which they claim the emergence of man on earth approximately one million years ago may not be acceptable to many. I myself have come across several research articles of scholars who while dealing with this subject have their own different views. In this regard I can particularly mention about F. Facchini's[2] research paper titled ***'Evolution, Emergence and Transcendence of Man'***. The argument given by archaeologists in support of the above scientists especially pertaining to the division of man's evolution by different ages may not be acceptable to some as we find other sections of scientists dealing with human affairs and archaeologists with their own different approaches. Even then their view is important and worth giving a thought.

Also a section of scientists dealing with the human affairs has proposed the argument that the place which holds evidence of man's emergence for the first time on earth is in the Indian Subcontinent; or it is today's India itself; or it was an Island which was a part of India that has now sunk into the Indian Ocean.[3] How much reality is there in the above argument of scientists, I cannot give any final comment because I am neither a scientist dealing with the human affairs nor an archaeologist.[4] However, upon studying different analysis of ancient Indian history, I can definitely accept the ideas that there has been a dwelling of man in Indian Territory since the ancient-remote period, and that from the ancient age India has had an exemplary, developed and harmonious civilization. And for this reason, I call upon scholars, researchers, or subject-specialists to come forward to analyze the arguments of scientists dealing with human affairs, anthropologists and archaeologists in which they present their arguments pertaining to emergence of man in India, Indian Subcontinent or an Island which was a part of India and now has sunken into the Indian ocean for the first time on earth.

During the digging work undertaken from time-to-time, such facts have come to light which both prove the presence of man on this piece of land for thousand of years, as well as the presence of thousand of years-old Indian Civilization. This digging work has not been done to the lower levels; yet objects found there have yielded interesting information about ancient India and a prosperous Indian Way of life in comparison to other cultures of that time. As a result, archaeologists have been called upon to undertake digs to the deeper levels so that the actual history of man in India can be known. Scientists dealing with the human affairs could then come to a concrete decision pertaining to the earliest Civilization of India.

Civilization, Culture and the Indian Way

Although many secrets pertaining to Indian Civilization are to be unveiled, particularly regarding man's emergence and the process of evolution, mankind has inhabited India since ancient times. In India there has been a rich civilization and culture full of many characteristics. It is evident from history itself. India's Culture received a wonderful and exemplary dimension particularly during the time of Dravidian-Aryan confluence. As a result of that confluence, Indian Culture appeared harmonious while maintaining its originality; it became a composite culture.

Full of harmony and composite characteristics, Indian Culture became the identity of India; it attracted the attention of the entire world. Through the ages there have been a number of ups and downs along the way, but Indian Culture remained largely intact. Today the average Indian is a follower of India's harmonious and composite culture. He is its nurturer; its protector. This is my firm belief.

Harmony and composite nature, the two unique and extraordinary characteristics, which manifested into multi-dimensions of the Indian Culture, and which gave a new identity to it around the world, also opened the door for the characteristics of many other cultures of the world; I firmly believe this also. Whether it is the matter related to contact with Greek-Culture and its influence four centuries B. C.; the contact with Shaka-Culture first century B. C. or in the same manner the entry of sacred Kushanas Characteristics, both harmony and composite nature have been responsible for it.

Furthermore, these two characteristics have also been responsible for making way for the entry of characteristics from the Huna-Culture[5], Heftal-Culture[6], Arabian[7] and other cultures, Mongol and European Cultures and their amalgamation with the Indian Culture. All these characteristics are today indivisible parts of the Indian Culture; they are part and parcel of Indians in one way or the other.

The Vedic-Hindu-View

Harmonious and composite culture, which has accorded a unique identity to India and which works for the expansion and development of the ***Samskaras*** of Indians according to time and space in the making of the Indian Way, is greatly influenced by the Hindu-View. In other words, the Hindu-View has its special and important place in the Indian Culture.

Hindu-view, simply put, is the idea based on ***Vedic*** Philosophy. In other words, it is a way of life directed by the ***Vedas***. The Hindu-View entered extensively and firstly in the life of Indians during the confluence of Dravidians and Aryans approximately 2000 B. C. or 4000 years ago. Universal acceptance and the welfare of all are central to ***Vedic***-Hindu View.

Of course there was a developed culture even before Dravidian-Aryan confluence; non-violence, planning and development and other characteristics were present in the ***Samskaras*** of Indians as evident from various articles found during the digging work of various cities of the time of the Indus Valley Civilization. However, before this confluence there was no uniformity in the social and religious life of all Indians living in different parts of India, i.e. from north to south and east to west. This uniformity definitely came into existence after Dravidian-Aryan confluence; and the

Vedas, particularly the guiding ideas in the ***Rig-Veda***, which later on came to be known as ***Hindu***-Views, played a decisive role in this context.

In the first ***Sukta*** of the first ***Mandala*** of the ***Rig-Veda***, God as the source of fire has been worshipped with the hope of His blessings for human-unity and the welfare of all; it definitely proves universal acceptance to be the nucleus there. In this very ***Sukta*** a keen desire for separation from the evil of violence[8], or in other words a wish for non-violence, is the indicator of those two great and exemplary values which defined day-to-day human practices from a ***Hindu*** or ***Vedic*** point of view. Moreover, those two values are even today the signs of their identity and will remain so in the future as well. Those two great values are: forbearance and tolerance.

Forbearance, full of the spirit of love and cooperation is that human practice which cannot be minimized to man-to-man relations; in its scope fall all living beings. Forbearance accords the highest level of morality to a human being; it develops ethics in him. Through it man takes notice of others' pains and their miseries and thus ultimately gives extension to non-violence that is ***Ahimsa***. If there are only two pillars of the ***Hindu***-View then the first of them is definitely forbearance. Without having forbearance in him no one can claim to be a ***Hindu***. If someone does so, then I have no hesitation in saying that he is a liar.

Tolerance is fully within the scope of patience; although like forbearance within it pervades not only the spirit of cooperation, but the fundamental principle to accept other perspectives. In other words, to acknowledge another's views, honour their ideas, as well as accept others' behaviour so long as they do not come in the way of one's own views, ideas and behaviours. Tolerance is the second pillar of the Hindu-View; in its absence one cannot claim to be a Hindu.

It was the tolerance of the Hindu-View which throughout time has offered shelter to those who were oppressed in their own countries and sought India for refuge. Hundred of years ago Jews, who suffered under Roman atrocities, reached Indian soil and received shelter. Parsis, the followers of Spitama Zoroaster found refuge here when their freedom was snatched away in their own native country of Iran. It is a long list of such refugees in which we may find the names of a number of human groups came from various parts of the world.

I am proud that due to the supremacy of tolerance, one of the chief fundamental principles of the Hindu-Views or Ideas, not only Dravidian-Aryans confluence persists in India but the blood of Shakas, Kushanas, Hunas, Greeks, Mongols, Tartars, Turks, Arabs, and Europeans is there in its land; that blood now flows through the veins of the harmonious and composite Culture of India.

I am also proud that India is the home of the followers of almost all major religious-communities of the world; they feel safe on Indian soil. Due to the tolerant nature of common people of India, they are assured of their existence here.

Gandhi: Hindu-View and the Indian Way

Mahatma Gandhi was himself a great Indian; he was an excellent Hindu. The Indian Way, in which universal acceptance is the nucleus of life and holds ***Ahimsa*** [non-violence] as the highest value for day-to-day practices, in which the Hindu aspect of tolerance is prominent, has not only been to the liking of Mahatma Gandhi in theory, he implemented it in his individual practices during the whole of his life as well.

The tolerance inherent in Hindu-View, which accepted all those social and cultural characteristics which landed upon Indian soil, and which opened the doors of self-expression and freedom for all in general and added new dimensions throughout time for progress and development in different walks of life, became the centre of attraction for Mahatma Gandhi.

Tolerance became the source of inspiration for Gandhi's thoughts and actions in India and for the international community. Regarding the aspect of tolerance in the Hindu-View, he went to the extent of saying:

"I have found it [Hinduism] to be the most tolerant of all religions known to me. Its freedom from dogma makes a forcible appeal to me in as much as it gives the votary the largest sense for self-expression." [9]

Not only this, Hindu acceptance developed on the basis of tolerance, which accords equal respect to others and which also calls upon man to honour another's faith, was largely appreciated by Mahatma Gandhi. For he said:

"Not being an exclusive religion it enables the followers of that faith not merely to respect all the other religions, but it also enables them to admire and assimilate whatever may be good in other faiths." [10]

The Indian Way does not consider views developed and established in different parts of the world to be inferior; the Hindu-View accords equal status to others' faiths, beliefs, and ways. As I have previously stated, it gives them an opportunity to be prosperous and calls upon coordination, cooperation and confluence with them. Furthermore, under its own shadow it nurtures them and accords defence and protection. Simultaneously, it invites them to broaden its scope and give strength to its composite nature.

India's Way is of tolerance; to accept other's characteristics and to accord them honour is its fundamental principle. That is why; being a great Indian, Mahatma Gandhi could perceive non-violence-an eternal, natural and primary human value-in all living faiths of the world; he could find it in the principal teachings of all the religious-communities as well as in the routines of all Propounders. In this context he clearly stated in the October 20, 1927 issue of Young India:

"Non-violence is common to all religions."[11]

In practice the quantity of non-violence can be more or less in different religious-communities. But non-violence is an eternal value; it is natural. Therefore, not a single religious-community could become indifferent of it. Not a single true religious teacher, incarnation, messenger of God or Propounder [founder] can separate him from it. Not only Buddhist teachings and Gautama Buddha, Jaina views and Tirthankaras, but Christianity and Jesus Christ, and Islam and Prophet Muhammad have also been consistently spreading the value of non-violence; and for this very reason they have been the great peace messengers in their own respective times.

Like Lord Rama, Lord Krishna, Spitama Zoroaster and Prophet Mohammed, Mahatma Gandhi considered

Jesus Christ also to be divine and holy[12]; he declared his teachings to be pervasive and important for the pathway to peace[13] and prosperity. Furthermore, he declared them sacred and welfaristic.

As the great religious teachers, incarnations or messengers of God, it doesn't matter where they were born in any part of the earth, their messages and teachings have always been for the welfare of the whole of humanity. Therefore, their teachings are the subject of adaptability for each and everyone according to time and space.

Along with this, they may become the basis of human unity and universal acceptance. They can strengthen the Indian Way, which is based on harmony and coordination as they have done in the past. Being an excellent follower and explainer of the Indian Way Mahatma Gandhi also accepted this reality. To quote the following line from one of his own statements appeared in the issue of Young India on November 24, 1927 about Gautama Buddha:

"He broadened its base; gave it a new life and a new dimension."

Whether the Christian spirit of service or Sikhism's heroism, or Islam's fraternity and belief in oneness of God, all these great characteristics had been the subject of attraction and adopting for Mahatma Gandhi. Through them he honestly accepted the reality of strengthening and broadening of the Indian way. In his column of March 21, 1927 to Young India, he specifically wrote about the contribution of Islam to the national Culture of India:

"Islam's distinctive contribution to India's national culture is its unadulterated belief in the oneness of God and a practical application of the truth of the brotherhood of man for those who are nominally within its fold. I call these two distinctive contributions. For in Hinduism the spirit of brotherhood has become too philosophized."[14]

Mahatma Gandhi's indication is clear. He desired the Hindu-View, which is the fundamental basis of the Indian Way and also the symbol of tolerance in theory and practice, to come out of the scope of over-philosophized spirit so that it could become conducive to the universal acceptance, which is the identity of India and for which Indians are known throughout the world. Is there any harm if for this purpose something is learned from Islam? It is of course welfaristic.

In the same manner if having intact their originality, in social, religious and other walks of life Indians adopt characteristics of others, as per the demand of time and space to broaden and strengthen the Indian Way then what harm in it? It is the century-old tradition of India; it is the basis of the fundamentals of the harmonious and composite Culture of India. Mahatma Gandhi gave a new dimension to it and thus he became the pride of India.

Conclusion

Change is inevitable. It is the law of life. Each and every origin and worldly thing, movable or immovable, is within the scope of the law of change. But how change becomes conducive to human progress and welfaristic to all living beings is the duty and responsibility of man himself. Man in an appropriate direction is capable of doing so. Whether it is the ancient past or the medieval period or the contemporary period mankind has done so at various levels and in different walks of life. I do not want to go into any details in this context here; we have before us the process of development of man right from the remote past which can prove this reality. Also the history of man can well prove this reality and that Indians through their prosperous way have played a vital role in this direction. In this way is the forbearance of human behaviours. This way is wide and is the carrier of tolerance. It is full of characteristics like harmony, coordination and compositeness and it is the nurturing of the Indian Culture. Hence, it is exemplary and adaptable.

Indians under the leadership of great representatives of the Indian Way have from time-to-time led the whole of the world. Gautama Buddha and Mahatma Gandhi were among those great representatives. Today the world is moving towards a new dimension. Unprecedented awakening, development and increasing steps towards globalization have presented before us a picture of ***Vasudhaiva Kutumbakam*** [whole world is but one family]. It becomes all-welfaristic, through it human-unity is established, for this we have our own responsibility. We must now clear our way by strengthening it; we must establish it at the world level. It is our foremost duty. If we do so, I am sure we will follow the path of Mahatma Gandhi also.

References:

1. Which is divided in three chief ages-Paleolithic, Mesolithic and Neolithic; and again Paleolithic and Neolithic in three each periods such as the first, the medieval and the last.

2. In which Facchini gives details pertaining to evolution, emergence and transcendence of man and also quotes theories of people like Darwin, Ayala etc. therein.

3. This argument is sound based on the results of a recent dig conducted by a team or archaeologists in West Bengal, who have declared it to be the first of its kind as well as perhaps the oldest in the country. According to the article which appeared in The Times of India, New Delhi on April 14, 2008, the dig-a treasure trove of cultural artifacts, fossils and cave inscriptions-is definitely significant as it cou!d yield a complete cultural sequence of early man. Located at Susuniya village, about 250 km from Kolkata on the banks of Gandheshwari river's tributary, the site was discovered a few days ago by a team led by internationally acclaimed paleontologist GI Badam, a senior consultant, IGNCA, New Delhi and Manbratha

Bhattacharjee, a professor of anthropology at the University of Calcutta. In his talk to The Times of India representative, GI Badam specifically mentioned, ***"A unique aspect of this site is that it exposes the uninterrupted cultural sequence of early man in various stages over a jungle area. Prima facie, we have dated this site to one million years to ten thousand years ago. It fits into the era between Paleolithic and Mesolithic periods."***

4. Particularly, when theories like 'that modern man spread from Africa throughout the old world, probably with some limited admixture with representatives of *erectus*, especially in southeastern Asia and Eastern Europe' are developed.

5. The Hunas reached India during the second half of the 5th century A. D.; why they reached India has nothing to do with my topic in hand; therefore, I do not want to touch upon this point. However, I would like to state that they along with Gurjars reached here. Both of them were brave tribes; like Aryans they too were skilled. They were hard-working; they made their harmony with the Indian Culture in the same manner as Shakas, Kushanas and Greeks had made before in the past. After their arrival in India the Hunas and Gurjars inhabited in Kashmir, Punjab, Sindh, Rajasthan, today's Uttar Pradesh, Gujarat, and other parts of Northwestern India. They not only adopted Indian custom, traditions and day- to-day practices but accepted almost all Indian Samskaras. The most important thing had been that they become identical to Indianness, or in other words they declared their identity as Indians which was a most pleasant situation. A section of historians considers today's Rajputs, Jats and Gurjars to be their successors. In these castes many great warriors and nationalists were born. Vallabhbhai Patel who is known as the Lion of Gujarat and the Sardar of India and who integrated and consolidated India on the larger scale is believed to be related to the Hunas and Gurjars caste as mentioned in the Bombay Gazette.

6. It was during the last decade of the 5th century A. D. when Heftals attacked India and reached its soil; although in comparison to Hunas they were not so influential.

7. Arabian Culture reached India through Sindh, which is now the part of Pakistan, in the 8th century A. D.

8. ***Rig-Veda*** 1-4, [Dayananda Commentary] ***"Agne Yam Yajamdhvaram Vishvatah Paribhurasi Sa Iddeveshu Ichchhate"***

9. India of My Dreams, p. 255 [***"I have found it to be the most tolerant of all religions known to me. Its freedom from dogma makes a forcible appeal to me in as much as its gives the votary the largest scope for self-expression."***]

10. Same as above.

11. Above.

12. Harijan, 6 March 1937 [Mahatma Gandhi writes ***"He (Jesus) is as divine as Krishna or Rama, or Muhammad or Zoroaster."***]

13. Young India, 20 January 1927. [He while writing especially about Islam mentioned, ***"I do regard Islam to be a religion of peace in the same sense as Christianity, Buddhism, Hinduism are. No doubt they are differences in degrees but the object of these religions is peace."***]

14. Young India, 22 December 1927

Bibliography:

- Gandhi, MK, An Autobiography or the Story of My Experiments with Truth, Navajivan Publishing House, Ahmedabad [India], 1957

- Gandhi, MK, Harijan Weekly, Published Under the Auspices of Harijan Sewak Sangh [1933-41]; by Navajivan Trust, Ahmedabad, [India], Between 1942-48

- Gandhi, MK, Hind Swaraj, Navajivan Publishing House, Ahmedabad [India], Reprint, 1958
- Gandhi, MK, Navajivan [Hindi], Weekly, Ahmedabad [India], 1919-31
- Gandhi, MK, Young India, Weekly, [1919-1931], Reprinted in 13 Volumes by Navajivan Publishing House, Ahmedabad, [India], 1984
- Manusmriti [Hindi Commentary], Randhir, Hardwar, Uttrakhand, India [Second Edition], 1988
- Max-Muller, F. and Oldenberg, H., Vedic Hymns, Part-First, Atlantic, New Delhi [India], 1990
- Saraswati, Swami Dayananda, Rig-Veda, Sam-Veda, Yajur-Veda and Atharva-Veda [***Bhasha-Bhashya***], Dayananda Sansthan, New Delhi [India], Year of Publication has not been mentioned.
- Sayana [Bhashya], Rig-Veda, Sam-Veda, Yajur-Veda and Atharva-Veda, Samskriti Sansthan, Bareilly, UP, [India], Revised Editions, 1996

****

2

India, Non-Violence and Gandhi

"The Rishis, who discovered the law of non-violence in the midst of violence, were greater geniuses than Newton. They were themselves greater warriors than Wellington. Having themselves known the use of arms they realized their uselessness, and taught a weary world that its salvation lays not through violence but through non-violence. Non-violence in its dynamic condition means conscious suffering. It does not mean meek submission to the will of the evildoer, but it means pitting of one's whole soul against the will of the tyrant."

-MK Gandhi

India: A Great Country

India is a great country. Its greatness is not in name only. India is an ancient civilization; its harmonious and composite culture is thousand of years old. India has been a leading nation in the fields of spirituality, science and arts for centuries; it has been accepted as a ***Jnana-Guru*** of the whole world. India brought the gift of the greatest, unique and adaptable concept of universal acceptance to the world; it gave the slogan of ***Vasudhaiva Kutumbakam*** to humanity. Furthermore, India gave so many matchless learned men, the ***Jagatgurus***, to the world, representing different branches of knowledge. The ***Light of Asia*** Gautama Buddha and the greatest initiator of ***Ahimsa Tirthankara*** Mahavira were born on Indian soil.

The greatness of India also lies in the fact that its land welcomed and offered refuge to all human beings from different parts of the globe. It did not matter if those people had their own religious-community, faith or different traditions or values; after reaching Indian soil they received a permanent abode without any discrimination. Resultantly, the followers of world's six major religious-communities dwell in India today[1] as well as people belonging to other religious-communities inhabit here.[2]

Besides Hindi, twenty-one main regional languages[3] are recognized by the Indian Constitution. However, one thousand six hundred eighteen languages are spoken by the people on a local level throughout India; these dialects are the medium of day-to-day practices of the common man. Furthermore, descendants of six ethnic groups are in India. Indian people celebrate twenty-nine major religious festivals. All those who stay on Indian soil are Indians; they are wayfarers of the Indian Way.

The Indian soil welcomes all. Indians see the image of God in a guest. Providing hospitality is one of the main characteristics of the Indian Way. The one who desired a permanent home on the Indian land not only received permission, but received opportunities to march forward on the way to progress as well. Those who assimilated India's values reached the heights of prosperity and became her own forever. Parsees, the followers of Spitama Zoroaster, who reached India from Iran approximately one thousand five hundred years ago, are the living proof of this.

Those who could not fully assimilate Indian values for whatever reason also became part of the Indian way. However, they did find themselves isolated; and they still find themselves in the same situation today. In comparison to others, they are far behind in progress and development. It is indeed a good lesson to be learnt by those who desire advancement while staying on the Indian soil.

India and Non-Violence

Ahimsa [Non-Violence], which is the first human value, is also a perpetual and natural value. It has played a vital role in India's greatness, especially from the perspective which I previously discussed. It is ***Ahimsa*** which accorded dynamism in the lives of Indians. It directs their day-to-day behaviours in such a manner that they can ensure their own existence; their conflicts, inevitable in daily life, are transformed and resolved. Moreover, it has given ever-new dimensions to the process of cooperation, the outcomes of which are present in the form of unprecedented and unending development in various walks of life.

Now, prior to discussing India and non-violence in-depth, it is necessary for us to clarify the meaning of ***Ahimsa*** and the main Indian concepts pertaining to it.

In Jainism ***Ahimsa*** has been analyzed minutely. The Twenty-Fourth Jain ***Tirthankara***, Vardhamana Mahavira, gave a unique dimension to ***Ahimsa*** through his own humanly practices, making it a subject of self-control, pure conduct and discipline. It is for this reason I have called him the greatest initiator of ***Ahimsa***. The essence of Jain ***Ahimsa*** lies in the following words:

"Complete aloofness from Himsa [violence] is Ahimsa [non-violence]."[4]

Clearly, Jainism brings ***Ahimsa*** within that comprehensive and extensive scope in which common man's entry is quite difficult. In it the smallest form of violence is accountable. Every form of violence, big or small, committed by a human being knowingly or unknowingly is worthy of consideration. Therefore, it is not possible for everyone to follow Jainism's brand of ***Ahimsa*** in the practical sense. Moreover, the Jain ***Ahimsa*** is completely based upon negative concepts pertaining to it. For this reason it also becomes impractical for the common man and can only be practiced by an initiator of a new age like ***Tirthankara*** Mahavira himself.

The ***Vedic***-Hindu Philosophy, which directs day-to-day practices of majority of Indians on the basis of guidelines, decided by the ***Vedas,*** particularly the ***Rig-Veda*** itself[5] considers ***Ahimsa*** to be an evil-free ***Dharma***. Of course, this ***Dharma*** establishes itself in the form of duty as well as goodness. Hence, along with not harming anyone by thought, speech or deed, and not depriving someone of life, relying for support of violence to maintain order and to accord justice is the basis of ***Vedic-Hindu Ahimsa*** [non-violence].

Although like Jainism, Buddhism also emphasizes

upon self-control, but generally it is not in favour of any such appeal in the name of ***Ahimsa***, which becomes impractical for the common man in his daily routines. Body-control, word-control and mind-control are the means of violence-control: they are the means of developing non-violence. Gautama Buddha called upon humanity to develop non-violence on this basis. He communicated the message of making ***Karuna*** [compassion]-a combination of comprehensive friendliness and pity-the basis of maximum possible human practices-a vehicle through which non-violence could be developed in all walks of life.

Some five hundred years ago, another religious philosophy arose on the Indian soil[6], which is known as the Sikh philosophy, and whose followers are known as the Sikh. As the Sikh philosophy came into existence in accordance with the Indian traditions and like Gautama Buddha, outlet of its founders and developers[7] was also from the followers of *Vedic*-Hindu religious-community, this philosophy also had deep impact of *Vedic*-Hindu philosophy on it; like Buddhism it accorded its due place to ***Ahimsa***. Like Gautama Buddha, all Sikh Gurus and Guru Nanak Dev in particular, emphasized upon pure and virtuous humanly deeds and self-control to pave the way for developing ***Ahimsa*** in man's daily practices. Furthermore, like Gautama Buddha who conformed to the prevailing conditions of his time by making ***Karuna*** the basis of developing ***Ahimsa***, Guru Nanak Dev, the first Sikh Guru, made harmony the basis of non-violence during his time and motivated people to regulate their actions according to it.

The four common points which we find in the context of ***Ahimsa*** [non-violence] in the four chief philosophies established and developed in India that played vital roles in making India great by strengthening the Indian Way are as follows:

1. Within the domain of ***Ahimsa*** [non-violence] are not only human-beings but all living beings;

2. In spite of being eternal, natural and the first human value, ***Ahimsa*** is a subject of practice according to the demands of time and space;

3. ***Ahimsa*** is an active value; it has nothing to do with cowardice as it is an ornament of the brave; and

4. ***Ahimsa*** is not a subject to be practiced occasionally; in theory and in practice it is all-timely.

Non-Violence and Gandhi

All the above four points, which are present almost with unanimity in four major philosophies-***Vedic***-Hindu, Jain, Buddhist and Sikh-which were established and developed in India, can easily be found in the Gandhian concept pertaining to ***Ahimsa*** [non-violence]. And, I would go to the extent of saying all the above four points are present overall in Mahatma Gandhi's ideas and practices-the centre of which is non-violence. Mahatma Gandhi brought a good harmony among all Indian philosophical concepts pertaining to ***Ahimsa***.[8] This clearly indicates that Gandhian non-violence is an excellent introduction to the Indian concept of ***Ahimsa*** overall. If someone desires to know and understand non-violence in India, he should do so by understanding the ***Ahimsa*** of Mahatma Gandhi.

Accepting those ***Rishis*** greater geniuses and warrior than Newton and Wellington who discovered the rule of ***Ahimsa*** in the primitive age, Mahatma Gandhi declared non-violence to be an active force.[9] Gandhi proved on several occasions that ***Ahimsa*** is not the meek submission before the will of the wrongdoer; rather ***Ahimsa*** is a fight using soul-force against the will of a tyrant which ultimately yields to victory. Through his non-violent actions, Mahatma Gandhi astonished the whole world.

For centuries it was the opinion of many in the world that ***Ahimsa*** was a subject limited to hermits of cave-dwellers. They believed that it was an individual matter and could be applied in the religious sphere only. Mahatma Gandhi, however, shattered this myth. He used ***Ahimsa*** in the political sphere and proved that it could be successfully applied in all walks of life and at all levels-individual, community, society, national and international-so long as the applier's intention is clear and full of honesty.

Gandhi spoke of achieving victory over the injustices of the world's mightiest empire through the non-violent actions of the individual.[10] And, as we know from history, his ambition was achieved. For confirmation, the whole series of events pertaining to India's freedom struggle under Gandhi's leadership[11] is before us.

In fact, for the first time in history, Gandhi added a new dimension to ***Ahimsa*** in theory and practice by working to unite the common men He established non-violence as a means, which could be most effective in the political sphere. By doing so, although he accepted not hurting anyone by one's own thought, utterance and deed, and not depriving of someone of life to be the supreme spirit of ***Ahimsa***, but he made the intent behind the act the acid test of it.[12] Hence, he removed the doubt that non-violence is a subject beyond the reach of the masses.

Mahatma Gandhi clarified the eternality of non-violence, and spoke of its naturalness before the common man. He expected the whole world and Indians in particular[13] to be as warriors and develop non-violence to the maximum possible extent. People should apply ***Ahimsa*** in their behaviours, ensuring their own personal freedom while securing freedom for all citizens of the world.

Indians have been capable of achieving this goal; history proves this fact. The main reason for India's capability is its people's commitment to non-violence. During the course of his non-violent actions Mahatma Gandhi too believed this, and on the basis of this he stated:

"India attracts me. It has everything that a human being with the highest possible aspirations can want."[14]

India is an ancient civilization. It has maintained its special place in the world, and today has its own identity and role to play. Without a doubt, India must march forward with the eternal and natural value of ***Ahimsa*** at its centre. By playing its role in international affairs it must lead the world, and on the basis of Mahatma Gandhi's following message it must transform the slogan of ***Vasudhaiva Kutumbakam*** into reality:

"I feel that India's mission is different from that of others. India is fitted for the religious supremacy of the world. There is no parallel in the world for the process of purification that this country has voluntarily undergone. India is less in need of steel

weapons, it has fought with divine weapons, it can still do so. Other nations have been votaries of brute force....India can win all by soul force. Poets have sung about it and seers have described their experiences." [15]

References:

1. Hindu, Muslim, Sikh and Christian.
2. Like Zoroastrian, Jews, Confucian, Bahai etc.
3. Asami, Bengali, Bodo, Dogari, Gujarati, Kannad, Kashmiri, Konkani, Maithili, Malayalam, Manipuri, Marathi, Nepali, Oriya, Punjabi, Samskrit, Santhali, Sindhi, Tamil, Telugu and Urdu.
4. Theory and Practice of Gandhian Non-Violence, page 3
5. The oldest treatise of the world and the greatest source of Universal Acceptance. Along with its first ***Sukta*** of the first ***Mandala*** many of its other ***Suktas*** clarify the significance and importance of ***Ahimsa*** [Non-Violence].
6. Guru Nanak Dev, who born in Punjab, was the founder of the Sikh Religious-Community. He, as the First Guru, also developed the Sikh Philosophy during the fifteenth and Sixteenth Centuries A. D.
7. Nine other Sikh Gurus in particular.
8. In this regard if we go ahead, we definitely find Gandhian non-violence bringing harmony among all concepts pertaining to it, doesn't matter if they are from the east or the west, or if they are ancient, medieval, contemporary or modern. Each and every one can find ***Ahimsa*** of his imagination in the Gandhian non-violence.
9. In the issue of Young India, dated 11 August 1920, Gandhi

wrote, *"The Rishis, who discovered the law of non-violence in the midst of violence, were greater geniuses than Newton. They were themselves greater warriors than Wellington. Having themselves known the use of arms they realized their uselessness, and taught a weary world that its salvation lays not through violence but through non-violence. Non-violence in its dynamic condition means conscious suffering. It does not mean meek submission to the will of the evildoer, but it means pitting of one's whole soul against the will of the tyrant."*

10. In his own words, *"Working under this law of our being, it is possible for a single individual to defy the whole might of an unjust empire to save his honour, his religion, his soul, and lay the foundation for that empire's fall or its regeneration."*

11. Between 1917 and 1942

12. See appendix-1 for details.

13. In this regard Mahatma Gandhi went to the extent of saying, *"I am not pleading for India to practice non-violence because it is weak. I want her to practice non-violence being conscious of her strength and power. No training in arms is required for realization of her strength. We seem to need it, because we seem to think that we are but a lump of flesh. I want India to recognize that she has a soul that cannot perish and that can rise triumphant above every physical weakness and defy the physical combination of a whole world."*

14. Young India, 21 February 1929 [Prior to it too on August 6, 1921, he had written in Young India, *"India is one of the few nations on the earth which have retained some of their ancient institutions although they have been overlaid with superstition and error. But she has hitherto shown an inherent capacity for purging herself of error and superstition. My*

faith in her ability to solve the economic problems that face her millions has never been as bright as it is today."

15. India of My Dreams, page 3

Bibliography:

- Andrews, CF, Mahatma Gandhi's Ideas, George Allan, London [United Kingdom], 1929
- Bhavan's Journal, Bharatiya Vidya Bhavan, Mumbai [India], [Volume-54, Number-17], April 15, 2008
- Gandhi, MK, An Autobiography or The Story of My Experiments with Truth, Navajivan Publishing House, Ahmedabad, Gujarat [India], Reprint, 1957
- Gandhi, MK, India of My Dreams, Navajivan Publishing House, Ahmedabad [India], 1957 and Seventh Reprint 1999
- Gandhi, MK, Harijan Weekly, Published Under the Auspices of Harijan Sewak Sangh [1933-41]; by Navajivan Trust, Ahmedabad, [India], Between 1942-48
- Gandhi, MK, Young India, Weekly, [1919-1931], Reprinted in 13 Volumes by Navajivan Publishing House, Ahmedabad, [India], 1984
- Galley, WB, Philosophers of Peace and War, Cambridge University Press [United Kingdom], 1978
- Kumar, Ravindra, Gandhian Thought: An Overview, Gyan Publishing House, New Delhi [India], 2006
- Kumar, Ravindra, Gandhian Thought: New World, New Dimensions, Kalpaz Publications, New Delhi [India], 2008
- Kumar, Ravindra, Religion and World Peace, Gyan Publishing House, New Delhi [India], 2007
- Kumar, Ravindra, Theory and Practice of Gandhian Non-Violence, Mittal, New Delhi [India], 2002

****

3

India's Concept of Peace and Gandhi

"If I want freedom for my country, believe me, I do not want that freedom in order that I, belonging to a nation which counts one-fifth of the human-race, may exploit any other race upon earth, or any single individual. If I want that freedom for any country, I would not be deserving of that freedom if I did not cherish and treasure the equal right of every race, weak or strong, to the same freedom."

-MK Gandhi

India's Status in World History

If we go through the pages of world history, we find India's status to be unique and extraordinary there. In India, which is a country of unity in diversity, human activities have been continuing since ancient times. Indians have been filled of enthusiasm. They, passing through the inevitable process of struggle and cooperation, have been giving dimensions to the development constantly. Furthermore, by strengthening harmony, one of the most practical aspects of ***Ahimsa***, they have been attracting the attention of the people of the world. Hence, they have been conveying adaptable message of peace to all-general and particular. Many pages of the world history are evident of those men and women who desired peace and in search of it they visited India from time-to-time. Influenced by the Indian concept of peace not only Greeks and Chinese, but many others too reached the Indian soil. They stayed here for months and years, studied the Indian Way in which universal acceptance is the central and reached back to their respective countries with exemplary and welfaristic India's message of peace.

Besides Chinese travellers Fa-Hein[1], Sungh-Yun[2], Hieun Tsang[3] and I-Tsing[4], or Greek travellers Megasthenese[5], Hippalus[6] and Kosmas[7], many others too from Central, Southeast, Southwest and other places of Asia visited Nalanda, Texla, Varanasi and Vikramshila, the renowned Indian centres of higher education, knowledge and learning in their respective eras. Indian Philosophy, knowledge and universal-acceptance based its way became the source of inspiration for all of them. Moreover, ***Ahimsa***-based practices of Indians and their goal of achieving peace attracted them the most. During their visits and stay they perceived India's concept of peace. They went to its depth and found it to be unique and exemplary.

Indian View of Peace

Now it is but natural to discern what the Indian concept of peace is. In fact, the roots of this concept could be found in that exemplary approach of universal acceptance, which developed centuries ago in India. Undoubtedly, the source of this concept has been the ***Vedic*** literature, and particularly the ***Vedas*** and ***Upanishads***. The development of this concept could also be seen in teachings of those philosophies which called upon the people to carry out their daily activities on the basis of ***Ahimsa*** and other values supplementary to it. Moreover, other philosophies too, it doesn't matter if they were developed on the Indian soil or they reached here from other parts of the world, more or less, strengthened the Indian concept of peace from time-to-time in prevailing conditions of the country.

According to the basic Indian concept of peace, or in other words from the Vedic point of view[8], by peace does not mean something static or perpetuation of the status quo. It has to do nothing with inactiveness. Also compulsion has no place in it. Rather, peace is an active force. It is dynamic. It offers that force to the individual, which develops the dynamic strength of the people to a degree that will enable to meet any situation. Peace creates enthusiasm in man; it brings a human being out of the domain of individualism and inspires him to do something more. The essence of the Indian concept of peace remains in the reality of 'achieving the goal'.

As I have already said, peace is not a situation of the status quo. Inactiveness and compulsion have no place in it. Therefore, it accords courage to meet all those odd situations which emerge at different levels of all walks of human life. It clears the way of progress. Those who try to connect peace with inactiveness and compulsion, or those who take it to be static, they are not correct. Rather, by doing so, they show their childishness. Such people, I have no hesitation in saying, neither know the meaning of peace, nor are they familiar with the Indian concept pertaining to ***Ahimsa***.

According to the Indian concept of peace individual is basic source of its creation and development. In other words, human being is the first centre of peace. That is why; activities, behaviours and practices of man are firstly responsible for the creation and development of peace. Thereafter, from individual to community-level is its furthering step. This very process has possibilities to further advancement and success in all circumstances. Therefore, from community-level to social-level and from national to international-level this process can step-by-step achieve the set goal. Eventually, the great idea of ***Vasudhaiva Kutumbakam***, which occupies the foremost place in Indian philosophy and the way, and which itself is the best dimension in the process of peace, can be feasible.

Those who hold basic knowledge of Indian philosophy, they are well aware of the fact that this philosophy makes ***Karmas*** [deeds] of a human being the basis of his fall and rise. A human being receives ***Phala*** [fruits], bad or good, according to his ***Karmas***. The Indian concept of peace too can be seen by connecting it with this idea of deeds and fruits of Indian philosophy. As it is known to all, human being has been accepted the centre of deeds by almost all branches of Indian philosophy-Vedic-Hindu, Jain, Boddh and Sikh. True and virtuous deeds of a human being create peace. They develop it and categorically and continuously grant extensions to its process. These very extensions are the furthering steps of peace as discussed already.

Gandhi as a Peace Initiator

Mahatma Gandhi was one of those great men of world history who were recognized as the true peace-makers in their respective times. As a peace initiator he received respect equal to Tirthankara Mahavira, Gautama Buddha and Guru Nanak Dev in India. At the world level he was also known as one of those who were busy in search of truth and non-violence; whose aim had been the establishment of peace on this earth. He was declared the second Christ by Romain Rolland.[9]

In view of great scientist Albert Einstein he was a man occupying the highest stage in a highly civilized society of imagination. He was fully capable of ending the cruelty by peaceful means.

In view of peace philosopher like Leo Tolstoy Gandhi was the best contemporary committed to morality and ethics. He was an expert of countering inhumanity by high human values.

Clearly, not only in India but in the whole world Mahatma Gandhi was accepted a matchless propagator of peace. He became a role model for his contemporaries and the generations to come. Through his peaceful efforts he inspired many in the world. In this regard the enthusiasm and activeness shown by him became exemplary for millions. And without a doubt in the root of that enthusiasm and activeness was Gandhi's harmony with the Indian concept of peace.

In his individual life Gandhi incessantly moved forward in search of Truth. Constant development of ***Ahimsa*** was the means of that search. And it was during the course of that search that he worked for the welfare of the common people, which was without a doubt a work for the establishment of peace. It was also a dimension on the way to peace. But, it was his greatness that after doing exemplary work for humanity he neither made any claim over this nor desired a credit for his work.[10] He simply said that he followed that ***Sanatana*** tradition of India which inspired a human being to carry out his/her duties for humanity. Furthermore, he called upon all, general and particular, to follow this tradition as he did. It was clear from that statement of Gandhi in which he had said, ***"My life is my message."***

After taking inspiration from the life and work of the Mahatma many people tried to follow his pathway not only in India but also in other parts of the world. They as per their ability and capability worked for the welfare of the people. And thus through their public services in different walks of life they proved themselves to be the makers and propagators of peace.

In these days of unprecedented development in all spheres we are witnessing an atmosphere which is full of uproar. Despite the increasing nearness at the global level we are observing rise in competitions. In the process of steady development it is not an unnatural thing. But increasing disparity amongst the people is a matter of concern. Furthermore, the hurting exploitation by one of the other is the matter of serious concern. This tendency of exploitation destroys that human freedom for which Gandhi had taken initiatives in South Africa and later in India, and which is essential for the establishment and development of peace. In this regard Mahatma Gandhi had said:

"If I want freedom for my country, believe me, I do not want that freedom in order that I, belonging to a nation which counts one-fifth of the human-race, may exploit any other race upon earth, or any single individual. If I want that freedom for any country, I would not be deserving of that freedom if I did not cherish and treasure the equal right of every race, weak or strong, to the same freedom."[11]

The above statement of the Mahatma, which in fact is the beginning anew of the Indian concept of peace, is a ray of hope. Also it is the best message for those who are engaged in their work for peace.

References:

1. As per the available evidences from history, Fa-Hien was the first Chinese Buddhist pilgrim who visited India. At the age of 64 he left for India in 399 A. D. and from India he returned back

to China in 414 A. D. In India, Fa-Hien traveled through northwestern parts; he especially visited, Kapilvastu, the birth place of Gautama Buddha, and Boddhagaya, the place of Buddha's enlightenment. He also visited Sarnath, the place of Gautama Buddha's first sermon; Kushinagar, the place of Buddha's Nirvana, and Nalanda, then one of the leading centres of study and research.

2. Sungh-Yun was another great Chinese traveler who visited northwestern parts of India, and especially to Uddiyana, [the Swat Valley] and Gandhara [Peshawar] in 518 A. D., i.e. the early part of the Sixth Century A. D. at the direction of the Empress of the Wei Dynasty to offer presents officially to the Buddhist sanctuaries and to bring back the Buddhist texts from India. He, after accomplishing his task, reached back to China in 522 A. D.

3. Hieun-Tsang [603-664] visited India between 630 and 664 A. D. during the rule of Emperor Harsha Vardhana. He was an outstanding Chinese scholar and his mission in India was a search of knowledge. Born at Ch' in of the Province of Hunan in China, he, at the age of 26, commenced his journey to India in 630 A. D. Apart from passing through the Valley of Kashmir, he traveled extensively to Texla [Takshashila], Mathura, Kashi [Varanasi], Kapilvastu, Kushinagar, Patliputra [Patna], Vaishali and Mahabhodhi. He also stayed at the University of Nalanda and traveled through some parts in Southern parts of India. Under the guidance of Shilabhadra and Buddhabhadra-the two renowned scholars-he gained knowledge; he studied subjects like logic, grammar, linguistics, medicine, crafts etc. He studied Vedas in details, collected valuable information and manuscripts.

4. I-Tsing visited India after Hieun Tsang in 675 A. D. when the Great Buddhist Emperor Harsha Vardhana had died and at that time India was in a process of political disruption; Buddhism continued steadily to declaim. Even then, before leaving back

to China in 685 A. D., I-Tsing visited Kapilvastu, Bodhgaya, Varanasi, Shravasti, Kanyakubja, Rajagriha [Nalanda], Vaishali. Kushinara etc. At Nalanda he studied Buddhism and Indian Philosophy in general and Vedic Way of life in particular. [Note: It is believed that Plato, a great Greek philosopher, who gave anew unity to ancient and scattered truth, and who is responsible to get Socratic Method of Education recognized, visited India. Alberuni, in his book on India has also mentioned about it.]

5. Megasthenese [350-290 B. C.], an ancient Greek geographer, historian and diplomat was appointed an Ambassador to the Mauryan Empire under Chandragupta Maurya whose period of rule remained between 321 and 297 B. C. Megasthenese authored Indica, one of the most popular work on India. He, during his abode in India, visited almost all northern India; he also reached Himalaya. In his effort to record the extent of the country, he reported that India's width from East to West was about 16,000 stages and its length from North to South 22, 300 stages [1 stage=180 meters]. In his work he mentioned about rivers of the country as Ganges, Indus and other 58 navigable rivers all over India.

6. Hippalus was a Greek explorer who visited India in 100 B. C. After his study about monsoons dared to leave cost and travel at strait line from the current M Pamp El Mantemp to Indus, in honour of Hippalus this winds were taken his name.

7. Kosmas, in his curious theories for earth, in which ground is level, is surrounded by ocean and after ocean there is paradise; and also in it in north there is a tall mount and Sun turns over it. In it there are important geographic material for the Red Sea, India Ceylon and places beyond them.

8. Which generally is known as the Hindu View today.

9. Gandhian Thoughts: An Overview, page 123

10. That can be well understood from his own statement in which he said, ***"I have nothing new to teach the world. Truth and non-violence are as old as the hill."***

11. Young India, 10 October 1931

Bibliography:

- Gandhi, MK, The Essential Writings, Oxford University Press, 2008
- Gandhi, MK, Young India, Weekly, [1919-1931], Reprinted in 13 Volumes by Navajivan Publishing House, Ahmedabad, [India], 1984
- Kumar, Ravindra [Edited], Global Peace: An International Journal of Philosophy, Peace, Education, Culture and Civilization... Volume 1-8, Number 1-4, Meerut [India], 2001-09
- Kumar, Ravindra, Gandhian Thought: An Overview, Gyan Publishing House, New Delhi [India], 2006
- Kumar, Ravindra and Gunn Alastair, Some Ideas on Civilization and Gandhi's Principle of Non-Violence, Centre for Civilizational Dialogue, University of Malaya, Kuala Lumpur [Malaysia], 2008
- Prabhu RK and Rao UR, The Mind of Mahatma Gandhi, Navajivan Publishing House, Ahmedabad [India], 1967

****

4

India, Gandhi and Relevance of his Ideas in the New World

"The whole gamut of man's activities...constitutes an indivisible whole. You cannot divide life, social, economic, political and purely religious, into separate watertight compartments."

-MK Gandhi

Introduction

In the whole world India is a country of its own kind. It is the only nation, which for centuries has been the centre of great attraction for the people of every part of the globe. On the strength of their knowledge and spiritualism, Indians have drawn the attention of the entire world. Its cultural values have left their deep impression upon the whole world. India's prosperity and the way of life of Indians have attracted a large number of people throughout the world.

Since ancient times, India has been a centre of rich and developed civilization. Many of its centres of education and learning have been universally renowned in their respective eras. Centuries before Christ, India had developed several high human values, and on the basis of them it kept its flag flying high. This country from time-to-time has given such world's mentors, who reached the highest stage of human status. They went beyond the nation's boundaries and became philosophical guides for the entire world. For their ideas and adaptable practices they are still ideal teachers for all general and particular, even after hundred of years have passed. Their ideas and works are capable of guiding the world even in current scenarios, if they are applied according to the demands of time and space.

Gandhi and Ahimsa

Mohandas Karamchand Gandhi gave a new dimension to ***Ahimsa*** [non-violence]-the eternal, natural and highest human value, in theory and practice. As the best and true representative of Indian Culture in his own time, Gandhi was a peacemaker's mentor. Like other mentors of the world born from time-to-time on the Indian soil, Gandhi's ideas and practices became equally adaptable in his own time for lacs and crores on the one hand, and on the other they proved to be a guiding force for people of many countries of the world. Particularly, they have provided guidance to those working for freedom and justice. Simultaneously, they are fully capable to guide the people today in a new world if they are applied accordingly. Furthermore, they will continue to do so in the times to come.

How? Before knowing and understanding it, we need to consider some fundamental points, and in this chain the first one is: What are the ideas of the Mahatma? Or, in other words: What is the philosophy of Gandhi?

In briefest, we can well understand the ideas or philosophy of Mahatma Gandhi in his firm belief in ***"mutual-dependence of man's activities on one other"*** and ***"unity of human-life"***, which is an indivisible whole. In his own words:

"The whole gamut of man's activities...constitutes an indivisible whole. You cannot divide life, social, economic, political and purely religious, into separate watertight compartments."[1]

Thus, Mahatma Gandhi believed that all human activities, essentially influencing each other, build ways for a life. In this regard, many philosophies also confirm the belief of the Mahatma. Intellectuals are well aware of interdependent development. These ways make the life of humans meaningful and effective, and achieving the goal of life such as Truth. The Mahatma called upon humans to come forward in such a manner. He, by doing so, also emphasized upon adoption of ***Ahimsa*** [non-violence], which is, as said already, the eternal, natural and supreme human value.

For Gandhi, non-violence is an active, pure and an eternal value for all times. It is the best means to reach the Truth. In other words, only through ***Ahimsa*** human life can be made meaningful with goal achievement. One can complete the mission of his/her life on the basis of it. Mahatma Gandhi had the firm opinion that except for non-violence, there is no other means to reaching a goal. Without ***Ahimsa***, one cannot obtain the Truth. In this regard Gandhi wrote the following in one of the issues of Young India:

"Means are after all everything. As the means so the end. There is no wall of separation between the means and the end."[2]

Thus, non-violence is the nucleus of Gandhi's ideas. In other words, his views revolved around ***Ahimsa***. And as mentioned, it is the only means to achieve Truth, and achieving Truth is the goal of one's life, or to get completeness of life. This must be kept in mind first of all by those who desire to be familiar with Gandhi's ideas.

In this chain, the second point relates to Mahatma Gandhi's actions. The actions he undertook on the basis of non-violence consistently gave new dimensions to his views. They made them firm and mature. Therefore, it is particularly necessary to know the intention which had been in the root of his actions.

Some people believed that most of the actions, if not all, taken by Gandhi were dedicated to the welfare of Indians. Indians were in the centre of his actions in South Africa and India. To ascertain the freedom of India and to accord justice to Indians were the prime objectives of his non-violent actions, some say. But this opinion is not based on truth. In fact, the welfare of all human beings was the spirit in the root of his actions. And in that context India was the main place of his actions.

This can be understood well through the actions undertaken by the world's other mentors, including Gautama Buddha, who launched their actions from their own respective countries, while keeping the welfare of the entire human world in mind.

If it was not so, the ideas of Mahatma Gandhi would not have been within the scope of philosophies like the following ones: ***"mutual-dependence of man's activities on one other"*** or ***"unity of human-life"***.

In this respect the third point relates to the refining of Gandhi's ideas according to the demands of time and circumstances of space. And this can be perceived well only through the series of events pertaining to three mass actions[3] launched to make India free from the British Empire. In this regard Mahatma Gandhi himself has written in one of the issues of Harijan:

"I am not at all concerned with appearing to be consistent. In my search after Truth I have discarded many ideas and learnt many new things. Old as I am in age, I have no feeling that I have ceased to grow inwardly or that my growth will stop at the dissolution of the flesh."[4]

It is clear that Gandhi's ideas, in spite of staying within the domain of non-violence, and even while adhering in search of Truth, are dynamic. They are the subject of modification and refinement as per the demands of time and circumstances of space.

Gandhi's Ideas in the New World

Two thousand five hundred years ago, Mahatma Gautama Buddha had said on the Indian soil that every creation and every object or thing, movable or immovable, was a subject of constant change. Besides Gautama Buddha, other great men too ratified this reality, directly or indirectly.[5] But it was only Mahatma Gandhi, who, after Gautama Buddha, proved this reality directly on the strength of his actions and thus made his ideas relevant during his own life time on the one hand, and he left the legacy of them as guiding force for generations to come on the other.

This is the main reason that even after more than sixty years of his passing away when the world has changed in different manners, almost all spheres of human life have turned over, and due to unprecedented development a new world has emerged, Mahatma Gandhi's ideas seem to be relevant; they call upon the anxious world to resolve newly created complicated problems in these days of unprecedented and suicidal progress and thus to lead the world on the pathway to peace. How? It is a question which naturally emerges in our minds. Having a practical approach in our minds let us analyze it!

We are well acquainted with the reality of those inevitable struggles and problems, which constantly emerge in our human world in all walks of life and at different levels. Without becoming indifferent to these struggles and problems we need to accept the reality of their resolution by ourselves. By doing so, if we are honestly ready to sacrifice in the twenty-first century, as sacrifice is a must in the Gandhian way, and go ahead with it, without a doubt, we would come upon wonderful results.

Firm determination is essential for sacrifice; a strong will is also necessary. Chivalry is needed for it. This is the call of the Mahatma and it is also the essence of his philosophy in the centre of which is non-violence-***Ahimsa***.

Without a doubt it is worth giving a thought. There is a need to adopt Gandhi's ideas in daily practices as per the demand of time and space. And while doing so, there is a need to introspect that without firm determination, strong will and chivalry, no concrete result could be possible. Only by doing so, the significance and importance of Gandhi's ideas in the new world can be perceived.

Ahimsa is the nucleus of Gandhi's ideas. Therefore, the adoption of non-violent means is compulsory in Gandhism. Gandhism calls one to Truth; it appeals to accept the real state of affairs, and without relinquishing self-respect, it urges readiness to compromise. There is no room for destruction of evil-doers in it. It expects the end of the evil. It promotes win-win situations for all the parties concerned, and not only for one party in dispute. It incorporates high morality in it and talks of good, healthy and welfaristic human behaviours. Now, ponder over it whether Gandhi's ideas and non-violent means suggested by him in resolving disputes, problems or struggles are relevant and capable or not in the new world?

Let us analyze the situation of the new world! These are the days of globalization. Today, not a single country of the world, it does not matter how mighty or rich it is, can think of its existence in a state of isolation. And since it cannot think of its existence as an isolated one, how should it think of development? If a country exploits the people of another country in such a condition, or snatches freedom of it, or oppresses it, then bearing the wide interest of the people in mind if other countries of the world take the way of non-cooperation with that country, it is not possible for it to endure such an action.

Non-cooperation has its important place in the Gandhian views. It is also an aspect of the Indian Way. But it needs extra care during its application in the international sphere. Moreover, it demands uttermost sincerity. Therefore, if under the leadership and guidance of the United Nations, which is a symbol of the Indian concept of ***Vasudhaiva Kutumbakam*** at the international level, any such action is taken with honesty, it will definitely prove to be effective. Also, it will be within the scope of Gandhian ideas.

As much as we take the course of non-violent means, we get ourselves nearer to Gandhian ideas. Hence, in all situations possibilities of non-violent means must remain. But when all such means fail, for protection of freedom and justice, if least possible violent means are applied in the larger public interest, it will not be a disregard of the Gandhian approach. Freedom and justice were supreme for Mahatma Gandhi. Therefore, he always advised to protect them if possible by non-violent means and if not by ***Ahimsa*** then by violent means.[6] But such violence must be momentary and by heart there should not be an ill-will towards the rival. Gandhi's brief statement, ***'intent behind the act'***[7] must remain present in mind during the course of indulging in momentary violence.

Mahatma Gandhi was an Indian-born world's mentor. Great Indian values, particularly the supreme value ***Ahimsa,*** were the central of his ideas. Especially, he desired solutions for all problems through the means of non-violence. His ideas based on non-violence are entirely important in the new world. They are completely relevant today and will remain so in future as well.

References:

1. Gandhian Thought: New World, New Dimensions, page 33

2. Young India, 17 July 1924

3. Non-Cooperation and Khilafat Movement [1920-22], Civil Disobedience Movement [1930-32] and Quit India Movement [1942]

4. Harijan, 29 April 1933; also appeared in the beginning of ***India of My Dreams***, under the title ***To the Readers*** [Note: In this regard he further mentioned, ***"What I am concerned with is my readiness to obey the call of Truth, my God, from moment-to-moment, and, therefore, when anybody finds any inconsistence between any two writings of mine, if he has still faith in my sanity, he would do well to choose the later of the two on the same subject."***]

5. Especially Vedic-Hindu, Jain and Sikh branches of Indian Philosophy are in unanimity on it in one way or the other. The youngest branch of Indian Philosophy like Sikh too called upon the people to pass through the process of his routines as per the demand of time and changed circumstances of space. The Sikh Philosophy and teachings, which are well compiled in the Guru Granth Saheb, are in favour of refining of old traditions and methods, established four thousand, two thousand or one thousand years ago, as per the demand of time and space. While doing so, they show full reverence towards old traditions and methods and talk of refining them only for the reason of their practicality in the modern times.

6. See Mahatma Gandhi's call to Indians on the eve of launching the world famous Quit India Movement in 1942

7. Theory and Practice of Gandhian Non-Violence, page 34

Bibliography:

- Gandhi, MK, An Autobiography or The Story of My Experiments With Truth, Navajivan Publishing House, Ahmedabad, [India], 1927
- Gandhi, MK, India of My Dreams, Navajivan Publishing House, Ahmedabad [India], 1957 and Seventh Reprint 1999
- Gandhi, MK, Sarvodaya, Navajivan Publishing House, Ahmedabad, [India], 1955
- Gandhi, MK, Young India, Weekly, [1919-1931], Reprinted in 13 Volumes by Navajivan Publishing House, Ahmedabad, [India], 1984
- Green, Martin, Tolstoy and Gandhi, Men of Peace: A Biography, Basic Books, New York, [USA], 1983
- Kumar, Ravindra [Edited], Global Peace: An International Journal of Philosophy, Peace, Education, Culture and Civilization... Volume 1-8, Number 1-4, Meerut [India], 2001-09
- Kumar, Ravindra, Gandhian Thought: New World, New Dimensions, Kalpaz Publications, New Delhi, [India], 2008
- Kumar, Ravindra, Gandhian Thoughts: An Overview, Gyan Publishing House, New Delhi, [India], 2006
- Kumar, Ravindra, Theory and Practice of Gandhian Non-Violence, Mittal Publications, New Delhi, [India], 2002
- Tolstoy, Leo, The Law of Violence and The Law of Love, The Unicorn Press, London [UK], 1959

****

5

India, Internationalism and Gandhi

"Through the deliverance of India, I seek to deliver the so-called weaker races of the earth from the crushing heels of Western exploitation. India's coming to her own will mean every nation doing likewise."

-MK Gandhi

India and its Culture

India is a country committed to internationalism. This commitment is thousand of years old. It can be well acknowledged and understood through India's ancient thought of ***'Vasudhaiva Kutumbakam'***. Along with this, thousand of years old Indian Culture, which is, undoubtedly, harmonious and evolutionary in nature, and in Gandhi's words has rich treasures[1], through the practices of its up bringers, Indians, has also been categorically reiterating its commitment towards internationalism. Till today it is doing so. Indian Culture along with its other unique and exemplary characteristics, of which adaptation and universal acceptance are the foremost, has been drawing the attention of the whole world by opening the door of the Indian land for each and every one, it doesn't matter to which part or region of the globe he or she belongs. This, without doubt, has been an outstanding step towards internationalism. For all the nations and citizens of the world it is a good lesson to be learnt. Particularly, in these days of globalization, which itself is a form of internationalism, and which is constantly decreasing distances among the nations at different levels and different walks of life, and in which marching forward together has become necessary, Indian Culture and its exemplary features can guide the world for the establishment of a true internationalism and also to make it firm and all welfaristic.

It was Indian Culture and its vast scope that accorded protection to the followers of various faiths and beliefs of the world from time-to-time. This Culture opened doors for all to settle on the Indian soil and provided equal opportunities for them to rise. This process started thousand of years ago and continued for centuries. Perhaps, such kind of exclusive and excellent work started in India alone.

India's Record of Non-Violence

India's commitment to internationalism can also be well observed in its respect to ***Ahimsa***, non-violence, the supreme human value. In other words, ***Ahimsa*** being an indivisible part of day-to-day practices of Indians calls upon human welfare at the highest level and thus makes the idea of internationalism firm and great. It works for human unity.

"Not to inflict others' thoughts, words and actions by our own thoughts, words and deeds, simultaneously not to spoil the life"[2] is included in India's concept pertaining to ***Ahimsa.*** In brief, ***"The aloofness in toto from Himsa-violence is Ahimsa-non-violence."***[3]

It is evident that not only human beings but all living beings are within the domain of India's concept of non-violence. Now, where there is such a feeling for all living beings, how much regard will be there for human beings? We can understand it from India's concept of non-violence and through it we can realize India's commitment and dedication to internationalism and universalism.

Indian philosophy, spiritual thinking and education, along with messages of those great men, reformers and initiators of new eras who were born on India's soil from time-to-time, called upon people to carryout their day-to-day practices having larger interest of humanity in the centre. They urged people to base their behaviour on the principle of ***'Vasudhaiva Kutumbakam'***. They declared nationalism to be the first stage of internationalism and inspired people to strengthen it with the purpose of prosperity and welfare of the whole world. Therefore, India's concept of nationalism has never been a narrow one, nor it has been ungenerous in its nature. It can be repeated undoubtedly that it was the early step towards internationalism. Those who consider Indian nationalism to be narrow in outlook or observe it to be isolated, they must understand its reality. They should go into its roots. If they do so, I am sure they will find it completely free from the state of isolation. They will definitely find it to be dedicated to internationalism or universalism.

Mahatma Gandhi, a great worshiper of ***Ahimsa*** and a forerunner of India's Culture in his time, had said:

"If I want freedom for my country...I do not want that freedom in order that I, belonging to a nation which counts one-fifth of the human race, may exploit any other race upon earth, or any single individual. If I want that freedom for my country, I would not deserve that freedom if I did not cherish and treasure the equal right of every other race, weak or strong, to the same freedom."[4]

This statement is fully capable of clarifying the reality of India's commitment to universalism. Simultaneously, his following statement is also equally relevant and significant in this regard:

"Through the deliverance of India, I seek to deliver the so-called weaker races of the earth from the crushing heels of Western exploitation. India's coming to her own will mean every nation doing likewise."[5]

Sarvodaya

Mahatma Gandhi's principle of ***Sarvodaya***, which is in consonance with Indian traditions and values[6] and which is also influenced by Ruskin's theory of ***'Unto This Last'***, can be considered to be the best on the way to human equality. This principle, without any caste, class, gender, community or territory-based discrimination, endorses equal value for the labour of an intellectual or a cultivator. It talks of the greatest happiness to all[7] in comparison to utilitarian theory of the greatest happiness to the greatest number. In it there is the room for equal opportunities for the lowest to progress. This firmly elucidates that the greatest happiness to all also includes the greatest happiness to the greatest number.[8] Hence, it brings the whole humanity in its fold and therefore reveals internationalism in a beautiful manner.

Trusteeship

Furthermore, Gandhi's theory of Trusteeship, which according to the Mahatma can be the alternative to the violence-based institution[9] like the State, clearly reflects the perception of internationalism. He as one of the great philosophical anarchists was in favour of abolishing the institution of the State step-by-step. In place of the State he stressed upon the establishment of a worldly order based on equality. It is in fact a step beyond internationalism. In it whole humanity without any discrimination and territorial limit comes together and becomes identical. Therefore, Mahatma Gandhi's views cannot be taken lightly, it doesn't matter if the institution of the State as desired by him cannot be abolished immediately or within a time fixed for the purpose. His views are worthy of consideration, it doesn't matter if his desire for a worldly order seems to be utopian to someone. In this regard Gandhi during his stay in South Africa had set an example of collective living in the

'Tolstoy Farm'. In that farm people belonging to different religious-communities, sects and castes stayed together. They worked, cooked and ate together. It was a successful experiment of Gandhi. Therefore, his ideas, in spite of seeming utopian or impractical and fully imbibed with morality and ethics, are the subject of minute analysis as they are important and significant for the establishment of internationalism.

Conclusion

Eighty-five years ago, in 1924, Mahatma Gandhi had said:

"The world desires today not absolutely independent States warring one against another, but a federation of friendly interdependent States. The consummation of that event may be far off. I want to make no ground claim for our country. But I see nothing grand or impossible about our expressing our readiness for universal interdependence rather than independence."[10]

This statement of the Mahatma adds to the concept of internationalism. It makes its range to be large.

It is possible that eighty-five years ago the above statement of Gandhi seemed just to be imaginable to many. But, today in completely changed circumstances of the world it calls upon us to think over it honestly and sincerely.

Due to constantly increasing process of development at the global level, despite the existence of independent nation-States, an advanced state of interdependence is before us today. This state will still go higher. It doesn't matter if it is considered to be a compulsion of the nations of the world, but to move forward together is inevitable now. Working together is necessary for all citizens of the world. In such a situation, suggestions of the Mahatma and views expressed by him from time-to-time, which are full of internationalism, prove their adaptability and significance. It will be better and welfaristic if nations of the world by having the views and suggestions of Gandhi in the centre come forward to work in a state of harmony as per the demand of time and space instead of working in a state of compulsion. In this regard if they create conducive atmosphere collectively and willingly it will do well to all in the world.

In the beginning we have discussed about India's commitment to internationalism. Mahatma Gandhi had desired India to come forward for the establishment of a worldly order dedicated to peace and prosperity. He also desired India to accomplish this gigantic task considering it to be her responsibility. It is possible because India, due to its unique values, exemplary culture and commitment to non-violence, is capable to do so. Therefore, India must come forward for the establishment of a true and real internationalism, and by doing so it must become ideal for others in the world.

References:

1. Young India, 1 September, 1921 [In fact in the end of his article entitled, ***'National Education'*** appeared in Young India on the date mentioned above Mahatma had written about India's cultural heritage. In this regard he mentioned further, ***"We have not known it, we have been made even to deprecate its study and depreciate its value. We have almost ceased to live it..."*** As Gandhi's statement is fairly significant until today, the whole text of the last paragraph of his article is included under the title Cultural Heritage of India in appendix–1]
2. Theory and Practice of Gandhian Non-Violence, page 3
3. Ibid
4. Young India, 2 July, 1931
5. Ibid, 12 January, 1928
6. Particularly related to the Vedic-Hindu View.
7. Young India, 9 December, 1926
8. Ibid
9. The Modern Review, page 412 [In this regard Mahatma Gandhi has written, ***"The State represents violence in a concentrated and organized form. The individual has a soul, but as the State is a soulless machine, it can never be weaned from violence to which it owes its very existence."***]
10. Young India, 26 December, 1924

Bibliography:

- Gandhi, MK, The Modern Review, Ahmedabad, [India], 1935

- Gandhi, MK, Young India, Weekly, [1919-1931], Reprinted in 13 Volumes by Navajivan Publishing House, Ahmedabad, [India], 1984
- Guha, Arunchandra, India's Struggle Quarter of Century [1921-46], Part I and II, Publications Division, Ministry of Information and Broadcasting, Government of India, New Delhi [India], 1990
- Kumar, Ravindra, Theory and Practice of Gandhian Non-Violence, Mittal Publications, New Delhi, [India], 2002
- Kumar, Ravindra and Gunn Alastair, Some Ideas on Civilization and Gandhi's Principle of Non-Violence, Centre for Civilizational Dialogue, University of Malaya, Kuala Lumpur [Malaysia], 2008

****

6

Gandhian Philosophy: Past, Present and Future

"India has still to attain social, moral and economic independence in terms of its seven hundred thousand villages as distinguished from its cities and towns..."

-MK Gandhi

Introduction

Mahatma Gandhi has been among those rarest personalities in the entire human history in whose theory and practice there is approximately unanimity. On the basis of his thoughts and practices, he attracted the attention of ***crores*** of his compatriots during his own lifetime. He became the source of inspiration not only for Indians but also for lacs of people of others countries after his passing away. After taking inspirations from the Mahatma, people struggled for certainty of their freedom. They became united and came forward for the establishment of justice. And on most of the occasions they succeeded. In this regard an account of at least one hundred struggles carried out in different parts of the globe during the entire period of the Twentieth Century can be presented. Among them the following non-violent actions launched between 1906 and 2000 A.D. are the most worthy of mentioning here: Women Suffrage Movement in Great Britain [1906-14], Résistance by Workers in Spain [1914], Demonstration against Constitution of British Protectorate in Egypt [1918], Students' Strike in China [1919], Freedom Movement in Korea [1919],[1] Polynesian Opposition to Rule of New Zealand in Western Samoa [1920], Resistance in Japan to Military Putsch by Non-Cooperation [1936], Sit down strikes in factories of France [1936-7], General Strike in El Salvador [1946], Resistance against the French Rule in Morocco [1950], Strike against United Fruit Company in Honduras [1954], Afro-American Campaign for Civil Rights, the Freedom Rides and the Birmingham Campaign led by Martin Luther King Jr. in the State of Albania to break down all forms of segregation in public places as well as racial criteria in hiring practices in local business in the United States of America [1955-63], Struggle for Bread and Freedom in Poland [1956], the students' stimulate civilian insurrection resulting in Pinellas's fall in Columbia [1957], Struggle for majority rule in Rhodesia [1960s], Struggle for independence from Central African Federation in Zambia [1959-4], the peasants' struggles in Pacora Valley in Panama and Peru [1962], the Grape workers' strike in Delano, California, USA [1965],[2] Women protest in Ottawa, Canada [1966],[3] the major action in Hue, Danang, Vietnam [1966], the students' demonstrations in Germany, Italy, Poland and Yugoslavia [1968], the protests involving workers, students and priests in Spain [1968-9], General Strikes in Italy [1969], the EDSA Revolution in Philippines [1986], the Zapatist Movement for National Liberation in Mexico [1996], and the people's struggles for the restoration of democracy in many countries of eastern parts of Europe during the last decades of the Twentieth Century.[4]

Moreover, people's interest and curiosity towards Gandhian philosophy in these days of constantly increasing process of globalization have amplified. The manner, in which people after taking inspiration and guidance from Gandhi's philosophy at all levels and all walks of life have become active to establish justice and secure freedom, proves the adaptability and significance of Mahatma Gandhi's philosophy. And the point of uttermost importance is this that people, besides becoming prepared for actions, have given dimensions one after the other to it according to the compelling demand of time and space and that too by staying within the range of the fundamental spirit of philosophy.

Now the basic question before us is that why people's interest and curiosity towards Gandhi and his philosophy is increasing day-by-day? In reply, we can say that to become familiar with this reality, it would be necessary to go into the pages of history to reveal how Gandhi, encouraged by ***Ahimsa*** [non-violence] developed his technique of resistance, namely ***Satyagraha***, first in South Africa with the purpose of getting those Discriminatory Acts and Laws repealed, which were particularly against the interests of Indian immigrants there. Simultaneously, we have to see that how did his technique acquire success in India and achieved freedom from the Colonial Rule? How, after Gandhi's passing away, his philosophy attained maturity and dimensions in social and economic spheres? Moreover, how his ideas proved their relevance for people around the world, in getting rid of atrocities and exploitation, and seeking justice at different levels?

Foundation of Philosophy

It is worthy of mentioning here that fully imbibed by morality and ethics, Gandhian philosophy incorporates those views of Gandhi which were developed according to demand of the time and space within the domain of non-violence. He was born in a Gujarati ***Vaishnava*** family. This family was committed to the Hindu-***Sanatana Dharma***, where truth and non-violence were considered as the ***Parmodharmah***. Furthermore, his mother Putalibai belonged to a family of ***Pranamis*** and had sympathy for Jainism also. In Jainism non-violence occupies supreme place. In it the smallest form of violence is accountable. Every form of violence, big or small, committed by a human being, knowingly or unknowingly, is worthy of consideration. Hence, his reverential belief towards ***Ahimsa*** started from his home and particularly from the teachings of his mother. Simultaneously, during his studies of secondary and post secondary level education, in spite of disparity in quantity, he found non-violence to be common to all religious-communities. This, without a doubt, deepened his faith in it. Furthermore, passing through experiences of life this faith increased in him to the extent that he arrived to the conclusion that non-violence was the law of life. Moreover, it was an essential condition of existence, progress and achieving the goal of life. Therefore, he made non-violence the basis of his ideas and actions. Hence, it can be said with certainty that in comparison to many other philosophies of the world Gandhian philosophy is not the outcome of an argumentation of high level. Rather, it is based upon true experiences of life. It is guided by the ***Sanatana Dharma*** and eternal values.

Application

The application of Gandhi's philosophy started in the last decade of the Nineteenth Century A. D. in South Africa. It constantly developed also there during the first two decades of the Twentieth Century. In both the cases, i.e. start of application and constantly development of his philosophy, the demand of time and prevailing circumstance of South Africa were also responsible.

Those who are familiar with life and works of Gandhi, they know that after his arrival in South Africa in 1893,[5] he, as an Indian, had to pass through some bitter experiences at individual level. In the root of those experiences were inequality, injustice and exploitation of immigrants. The policies adopted by the then Colonial Government of South Africa in the name of racial discrimination towards Asians in general and Indians in particular were responsible for that. And this was the reason of transformation of Gandhi's philosophy into the action. His actions constantly and successfully carried out on the basis of non-violence better known as ***Satyagrahas***. They were the source of evolution of his philosophy.

Gandhi stayed in South Africa for about 21 years between 1893 and 1914. During his stay, he successfully launched actions to abolish ***'The Indian Franchise Bill'***, ***'The Black Act'***, **'The Immigration Act'**, 'The Pound 25 Tax which was later reduced to Pound Three' and such other provisions which were unjust. Thus, he could propose an effective philosophy to the world, which after its due modification and purification according to the demand of prevailing circumstances of India, again proved to be significant and welfaristic.

Through more than one dozen ***Satyagrahas*** carried out between 1918 and 1942, under the guidance and leadership of Gandhi himself, and some of his prominent comrades,[6] an unprecedented wave of awakening in social, political and economic spheres of India emerged. It was that very awakening in the masses which made India politically free from centuries old slavery, particularly the Colonial Rule

Mainly in three stages, i.e. through the Non-Cooperation [1920], the Civil Disobedience [1930]7 and the Quit India Movement [1942], Gandhi carried out his non-violent actions with the complete involvement and participation of the masses. Through them he made his compatriots conscious of their rights of freedom and equality and thus led them to the room of independence. Later, his actions in India became exemplary for the whole world. They also became the basis of adaptability and significance of Gandhian philosophy.

Socio-Economic Aspect

So many pages of history of India and the world well maintain the account of non-violent actions of Gandhi. Therefore, it will not be contextual if anything more is mentioned here in that regard. But, the application of Gandhian philosophy which revealed through the Bhoodan Movement in the sixth decade of the Twentieth Century was definitely astonishing in India, a country of diversities. Undoubtedly, the Bhoodan Movement gave a new dimension to Gandhian philosophy. Furthermore, it confirmed his philosophy to be a philosophy of peace and prosperity. It can be said so firmly because the Bhoodan Movement had two chief aims:

1. To accord social justice to those Indians who were unprivileged for centuries; and

2. To provide equal opportunity to people to become self-dependent in the economic field

Although India achieved its political independence from the Colonial Rule in the year 1947, but thousands and lacs of its citizens were still under the clutches of massive dissimilarity in social and economic fields. They were landless in India, a country where agriculture was, and is, the backbone of the society and economy. That is why; despite becoming political free a large number of people in India looked upon those opportunities which could lead them towards self-reliance. It was but natural. In a country like India where people are not provided equal opportunities in social and economic fields, each and everyone does not become a part of development, prosperity and peace, in spite of political freedom, would remain only a dream. Obviously, peace is not a thing set in a particular place. Development is connected with it. It is not limited just to a 'word'. Peace is an active force. It is a subject of practice. Gandhian philosophy itself discloses this fact.[8]

Therefore, by giving an unprecedented dimension to the application of Gandhian philosophy in social and economic spheres, and that too according to the demand of time and space, the Bhoodan Movement became a commendable non-violent action. The significance of this action remained in the fact that it had no direct or indirect observation of Gandhi and it was successfully carried out after his passing away. It categorically paved the way for application of Gandhian philosophy in above-mentioned fields.

In India, without a doubt, the Bhoodan Movement also became ideal because it opened the doors for application of an important aspect of Gandhian philosophy known as ***Sarvodaya***.[9] Fundamentally based upon ***Sanatana*** opinion that "***All ...belongs to Gopal [God]***", the ***Sarvodaya*** is a doctrine developed by Gandhi after becoming influenced by the work entitled, 'Unto This Last',[10] by John Ruskin[11]. This book of Ruskin is a basic work of Christian Socialism. In it John Ruskin, the author, takes the following from a statement of the Jesus in the parable of the labourers in the vineyard, ***"I will give unto this last, even as unto thee."***

Ruskin himself was an ardent supporter of equality for all. He was of the opinion that no one should be exploited in society. Everyone should be given equal opportunity to rise in the social field. ***Unto this last*** was his ideal. The essence of it could be observed from the following three points:

1. The good of the individual is contained in the good of all;

2. Lawyer's work has the same value as the barber's in as much as all have the same right of earning their livelihood from their work; and

3. The life of the labour, the life of the tiller of the soil and the handicraftsman is the life worth living.

After adopting the above three principles in his life, Gandhi, as mentioned, developed the doctrine of ***Sarvodaya***. He made his mind to apply this doctrine on a wider scale after India's political freedom from the Colonial Rule. It was evident from a new draft which he prepared for the Indian National Congress on January 29, 1948, a day before his death. In that draft he had clearly mentioned, ***"India has still to attain social, moral and economic independence in terms of its seven hundred thousand villages as distinguished from its cities and towns..."***[12]

But, unfortunately, he was assassinated on January 30, 1948. Thus, without applying his doctrine at a wider scale he left it as legacy for his compatriots and particularly his successors. It was Vinoba Bhave[13], his first ***Satyagrahi*** of the Individual ***Satyagraha*** [1940] and one of his closest disciples, who after Mahatma Gandhi's passing away carried forward his ***Sarvodaya*** mission through the ***Bhoodan*** as its first step.

As history is evident, the Bhoodan Movement was started by Vinoba Bhave from Pochampalli, the first village of Telangana region of the present Andhra Pradesh, in April 1951. Why? There was a reason to do so from that very region. In fact, before the dawn of independence of India in 1947 the law and order situation was very critical in the whole of the Telangana region. There was a clash of severe nature between the landlords and the landless over the occupation of land. The landlords occupying most of the land were rich. Contrary to it, the landless, despite the vast majority of population, were poor and backward. Undoubtedly, unjust distribution of land in India was responsible for it. Hence, landless had become violent. Many of the landless were influenced by the Communists. Therefore, controlling their violent attacks on the landlords had become a serious challenge for authorities. Many of the landlords had to flee from the region to other places for their safety. The situation could improve only after the freedom of the country and particularly after the merger of the State of Hyderabad into the Indian Union.

Vinoba Bhave was well acquainted of this problem. He was of the firm opinion that this serious and complicated problem could be solved by goodwill, which, of course is the nucleus of Gandhi's philosophy and for it, ***"...Removal of unjust distribution of land in a peaceful way is [absolutely] necessary."***

Therefore, it was decided to launch the Bhoodan Movement from Pochampalli. Vinoba Bhave started his journey to that village. On the way he reached the Central Prison of Hyderabad on April 15, 1951 as goodwill gesture to meet those Communists who were imprisoned due to their involvement in anti-social activities and provoking violence in the Telangana region.

Soon after reaching Pochampalli on April 18, 1951, Vinoba Bhave started open dialogue with the landless Harijans of the village. The process continued further in an atmosphere of goodwill and in the presence of the landlords. During that course of dialogues Harijans told Vinoba Bhave, ***"If they get only eighty acres of land, they will cultivate it and eke out their living."***

Hearing this, Acharya Vinoba Bhave pondered over it. After some time imploring people present there he asked if anyone could give away the land as gift [Bhoodan] for the purpose! A Zamindar named C. Ramachandra Reddy immediately declared donation of his one hundred acres of land instead of eighty acres. It was astonishing for the Acharya. He considered it as 'Divine Revelation'. He also saw in such kind of voluntary donation of land the possibility of resolving centuries old problem of millions of the landless agricultural labour.

So, from Pochampalli, the great work of voluntary donation of land, the Bhoodan, started successfully. The Acharya stayed in the Telangana region for about a month and a half and collected 12,001 acres of land as donation. Before leaving the region he constituted a committee of locals to distribute the gifted land among the landless. Hence, this was the early phase of the first step of the

Bhoodan Movement, an application of Gandhi's philosophy in social and economic spheres of India.

The second phase of the Movement started in 1952 during Acharya's long journey on foot along with his companions from Pawnar Ashram to Delhi, which lasted for nearly two months. Asking for gift of land from landlords Vinoba and his colleagues reached Delhi. In that journey, giving extension to this programme, Vinoba Bhave started asking for ***Sadhanadan***[14], ***Shramadan***[15] and ***Gramdan***[16], in which considerable success was recorded.

From Delhi the Bhoodan Leader and his co-workers entered the province of U. P. followed by Bihar and from both the provinces, besides ***Sadhanadan***, ***Shramana***, and ***Gramdan***, they also got hold of 2, 95, 028 and 22, 00,000 acres of land in gift respectively. Later, they, under Vinoba Bhave's leadership reached Orissa via West Bengal and there they got 812 villages in donation. Similarly, in Tamilnadu 175 villages were given in donation. Kerala, Karnataka, Maharashtra, Jammu and Kashmir and other provinces also followed Tamilnadu and there also many villages were given in donation. On the whole in a country like India, under Vinoba's leadership such a great work was started on Gandhian principles which helped in paving the way for a peaceful and bright future for millions of landless people working hard day and night.

Vinoba Bhave wanted approximately 1/6 part of the entire agricultural land of India[17] to be gifted so that it might be distributed amongst those who were landless. And thus through it a new society on the basis of non-violence could be built in which all people could advance towards prosperous and peaceful life. In Vinoba's own words, ***"We seek to reconstruct society on a new basis. That is the purpose behind the Bhoodan work...What we want to establish are new values-to make morality the guiding principle of social life and to make economics, which enjoys undue importance at present...The Bhoodan Movement is for us an instrument for achieving a non-violent and peaceful change of values [as per the demand of time]."***

Thus the application of Gandhian philosophy in social and economic fields could disclose before the whole world through the Bhoodan Movement in India. After experiments of Gandhi's philosophy in political sphere during his own time, it paved the way for many peaceful actions carried out in social and economic spheres around the world in general and in India in particular. To become familiar with a complete account of those actions in India only, we need to produce volumes. But, here it is enough to hold that until today the relevance and significance of Gandhian philosophy in accordance with demand of time and space seems intact.

Current Perspectives

Although from the series of events in which during the last one decade people around the world in general, and India in particular, have come forward to bring changes in various walks of life, or to bring justice through non-violent actions, or in other words through Gandhian way, itself proved relevance of it, but if we analyze some of the known events here it will not be out of context. We know that after the evolution of Gandhian philosophy in political, social and economic fields under Gandhi's guidance himself, and later mainly through the Bhoodan programme, the process of its application has been continued in India and all over the world. In this regard the role of some of the women, who came on the forefront to lead non-violent actions especially during the second half of the last century and in the beginning of the twenty-first century, has been extraordinary and noteworthy.

In this regard the non-violent struggle of Aung San Suu Kyi against the ruling Junta- military dictators of his own country, in Burma-Myanmar, since 1988 is one of the living examples before us. Aung San Suu Kyi launched agitation for the restoration of democracy in 1988 at the time when local military rulers of Burma denying it deprived the people of their rights. They started suppressing people forcefully. Resultantly, Suu Kyi was arrested in 1990 under the 'State Protection

Act-1975'. This Act grants the government the power to imprison persons for up to five years without a trial. But from the Jail she continued inspiring people to fight against injustice. She took the course of several Gandhian methods of protests including the fast unto death.

Since May 30, 2003 Aung San Suu Kyi is completely under house arrest. Now, she has no direct contact with her compatriots. No visitor is allowed to her except government appointed physician and one or two more people. But still she is the ray of hope for thousands of those Burmese who from time-to-time come forward to challenge the ruling Junta non-violently. Through their actions they attract the attention of all those who are concerned of equality, freedom and justice. Aung San Suu Kyi, without caring for individual sufferings, and making sacrifices for the humanity, has shown chivalry for the last twenty one years [1988-2009]. Hence, she has become the source of inspiration for many in Myanmar and other countries of the world as well.

Sharmila Chanu, another woman from Manipur, India, is demanding amendment in the 1972 Armed Forces Special Powers Act, known as the AFSPA. For it, she is struggling since November, 2000. She has emerged as one of the leading activists engaged in applying Gandhian philosophy during the last one decade. The AFSPA Act grants the armed forces down to the rank of a non-commissioned officer, the power to shoot and kill, to enter and search and arrest without warrant, any person against reasonable suspicion that exists that he has committed or is about to commit a cognizable offence in the northeastern provinces of India in Manipur. When on November 20, 2000 twenty ordinary people were killed by the armed forces under the provisions of this Act Sharmila Chanu went on indefinite fast demanding repeal of the AFSPA. Hence, she took the course of Gandhian ***Satyagraha***. Resultantly, for the charge of making effort of committing suicide, Chanu was arrested under section 309 of the Indian Penal Code. Still she is under detention. Some times in the All India Institute of Medical Sciences of Delhi and some times in the Jawaharlal Nehru Hospital of Imphal liquid is injected into Chanu's body forcefully. However, she is firm on her way. Still she is on fast and struggling non-violently. Hence, her determination and techniques of actions attract attention of many of those who are concerned for human values and desire their re-establishment through non-violent methods.

Both these women have not yet recorded victory through their non-violent actions. However, the manner they have come forward by applying Gandhian philosophy to counter injustice and atrocities that is mentionable. Hopefully, both of them should achieve success sooner or later. Gandhian philosophy conveys the message of becoming adherent to truth and with truth to march forward without apprehension. As both of them have been following this message and they have been in action for years, there is possibility of their success in one way or the other.

Another two women-Ila Bhatt and Vandana Shiva[18], through their respective organizations, namely the Self Employed Women's Association, the ***SEWA***, and the ***NAVDANYA***, are carrying out noteworthy constructive activities in social-economic field of India for the last more than three decades.

The ***SEWA***, a non-government organization of Ahmedabad, Gujarat, is functioning for the upliftment of women. Micro finance management through the ***SEWA*** Bank, which provides loans to women and allows them to set up bank accounts in their names, is the central of the activities of this organization. Moreover, activities related to cooperative work, particularly collection of the milk by women is also carried out by this organization. As its furthering step the ***SEWA*** has recently expended its activities in the form of solution to the labour problem. Resultantly, today a strong community of more than three hundred thousands women works tirelessly and with enthusiasm in its supervision to create self-reliance in them. Hence, the important work of the ***SEWA*** can be the source of inspiration for those desired to go forward in this direction.

Promotion of biodiversity conservation, organic farming and process of seed saving are among the main activities being carried out by the *NAVDANYA*, a leading voluntary organization for more than three decades in India. Mahatma Gandhi has given priority to constructive works in his programmes regarding reconstruction of society. In it the protection of natural resources occupies prominent place. This organization is engaged in carrying out these activities accordingly. Moreover, through these activities this organization is functioning for the awakening among the rural masses and particularly for the progress of the peasantry of India.

In brief, works being done by the ***SEWA*** and the *NAVDANYA*, as constructive activities, are the methods of social change in India in one way or the other. They can be considered experiments of Gandhian philosophy according to the demand of time. These kinds of functions can be ideal for those non-government organizations that are engaged in working to improve women's condition or struggling for their upliftment, and especially where rural masses and agriculture play vital role in people's development.

By applying Gandhi's peace philosophy in prevailing circumstances many others are also engaged in their work for the welfare of humanity not only in India but also in other parts of the world. In this regard the name of Julia Butterfly Hill, a known American activist and environmentalist, who is best known for living on a 180 foot tall six hundred years old California Redwood tree for 738 days, between 10 December 1997 and 18 December 1999, can be mentioned here. As known to many, Julia lived barefoot on the tree, known as '***LUNA***' to prevent loggers of the Pacific Lumber Company from cutting it down. Julia's work can be compared with many other leading environmentalists who have been engaged in their work of saving natural resources individually as well as collectively.

It is a long list. If along with internationally renowned people like environmentalist Sunderlal Bahuguna and activist sociologist Bindeshwar Pathak, the names of others who are carrying out exemplary activities as per the demand of time are included, it will become too long. Therefore, it is enough to learn that a large number of people engaged in various activities in all walks of life and at different levels through their respective organizations and institutions they are working day and night. It clarifies that thousands of people are trying to carry out their activities pertaining to human welfare more or less on the basis of Gandhian philosophy. They, by adopting refined non-violent methods, which can be applicable in prevailing circumstances, are indulged in work for development and prosperity of common man, and through this in creating a culture of peace. Only in India there are one hundred such Gandhian organizations and institutions.[19] The Banwasi Sewa Ashram [Uttar Pradesh], the Gandhi Peace Foundation [New Delhi], the Gandhi Peace Foundation Trust and the Andhra Mahila Sabha [Andhra Pradesh], the G. R. Institute of Non-Violence [Kerala], the Institute of Gandhian Studies, Wardha [Maharashtra], the Mahatma Gandhi Centre, Coimbatore [Tamilnadu], the M. C. Mehta Environmental Foundation [New Delhi], the Rashtriyashala, Rajkot [Gujarat], the Sampurna Kranti Vidyalaya [Gujarat], the Sarvodaya International Trust, Bangalore [Karnataka], the Saurashtra Rachnatmak Samiti, Rajkot, [Gujarat] etc., which accepting the inevitability of the 'Law of Change', and without compromising with the principle of ***Ahimsa***-the fundamental basis of Gandhi's philosophy, are carrying out their activities.

In this regard important and welfaristic works being done by the 'Anandawana Ashram' of Baba Amte[20] for treatment and rehabilitation of leprosy patients, the disabled and other people from marginalized sections of society in the remote and economically less privileged district of Chandrapur in Maharashtra and also for environmental awareness and wildlife preservation, the 'Sulabh International Social Service Organization'[21] the 'Gram Sewa Samaj'[22], the 'Vedachhi Pradesh Sewa Samiti'[23], the 'Sarvodaya Parivar'[24], the 'Gandhi Vidyapeeth Vedachhi'[25], and the 'Sarvodaya Mandal[26] are worth mentioning. All activities of these organizations and institutions which are being carried out for the tribal people, farmers, labours and the rural masses, and of which this writer himself is a witness, encourage people to re-evaluate the adaptability and relevance of Gandhian philosophy in the current perspectives. Furthermore, possibility of application of Gandhian philosophy in the prevailing circumstances can be testified from activities of these organizations and institutions.

Future Perspective

Gandhian philosophy, as mentioned in the beginning, is not the outcome of an argumentation of high level. Rather, it is guided by ***Sanatana Dharma***. By staying within the domain of non-violence, it is dedicated to the welfare of all, general and particular. It can be called the philosophy of the common man. This philosophy has a direct appeal for all. Therefore, there can always be a possibility of its application. However, those who wish success through this, they need to follow certain things. Those things can be considered essential conditions for the success of Gandhian philosophy. What are those conditions? Before clarifying it, it will be contextual to mention here something about those non-violent actions, which have been carried out recently in the name of Gandhigiri.

Inspired by some of the illustrations of a feature film released sometime back in the name of 'Lage Raho Munnabhai'[27], some people have tried to set examples making them the basis of their non-violent actions to get rid of injustice being done on them. Particularly, people have come forward to resist against the injustice in the name of Gandhigiri.[28] They have done so non-violently and on most of the occasions they have recorded victories. Gandhigiri has been named as ***Satyagraha*** by them. Many people have declared it to be an effective method of Gandhi's philosophy in changed circumstances of the Twenty-First Century. They have explained Gandhigiri in the following manner: 'Gandhi'=Gandhi, the Mahatma, and 'Giri'=the way. This, according to them, is the way to end forcibly inflicted injustice. Therefore, it is a kind of ***Satyagraha*** or in other words application of Gandhian philosophy. And, as said already, on most of the occasions their actions as Gandhigiri have became successful.

During the month of October, 2006, some doctors and students made Anbumani Ramadoss, then the Union Minister of Health and Family Welfare of the Government of India, ashamed for not taking a strong action on the issue of the Dengue Fever which claimed 26 lives in Delhi alone. During that very month some writers proposed reforms to the educational system by using Gandhigiri as a concept in Karur, Maharashtra.

Carpenters in Gujarat practiced it to make sure flaky clients paid up for services they rendered. Peasants of Maharashtra used it to make those officers of the provincial government ashamed who were not ready to sanction loans to farmers in drought-ridden areas. In all these cases people adopted methods like offering flowers, lightening the candles and demonstrating peacefully. In the year 2007, an old man[29] taking the course of Gandhigiri registered protest at the Akota Provident Office after becoming tired of running pillar to post for provident fund money from that office. In Hyderabad a section of doctors adopted it against atrocities of a local M. L. A., first by forming a human chain and later by offering petrol to spray it and set them on fire.

This process continued further. Besides, Allahabad, Chandigarh, Delhi, Patna, Pune and Vishakhapatnam, practices of Gandhigiri were reported from London, UK and Washington DC, USA. People adopted this method against their own unjust arrest or of others' acquainted to them. They chose this method in regard to security of their jobs, sanitation and water-supply management work in cities. In almost all cases came to the light in the name of Gandhigiri justice-seekers or protestors have been non-violent during their actions. It can be considered a matter of great satisfaction. Along with this, they have, more or less, tried to apply this method after ascertaining the prevailing circumstances. In fact, both these factors have been responsible for the success of all actions of Gandhigiri. In spite of not agreeing with those who take Gandhigiri to be synonymous of ***Satyagraha***, as egoism can be seen in the word Gandhigiri, which has no place in Gandhi's philosophy, for people like me it can be a matter of satisfaction that in the actions taken through this method activists have tried to be committed to non-violence. And as mentioned already, they have been ascertaining to the prevailing circumstances. I wish further purification of this method adopted in the name of Gandhigiri so that it could completely come within the range of Gandhian philosophy to prove its importance and relevance.

Now, before putting a full stop to this discussion it is obligatory to arrive to a conclusion suggesting some points, which can be the directives for the success of Gandhi's peace philosophy in a completely changed world of the day and also in the future.

Gandhian philosophy, I repeat, despite its development on the basis of non-violence, is not static. Rather, it is dynamic. Its basis, non-violence, itself is a subject of purification according to time and space. Therefore, those who desire success through applying Gandhian philosophy, they must go forward only after bringing it into harmony with prevailing circumstances and demand of time. This is the first condition of its success.

Contrary to Utilitarianism, which believes in the idea of the greatest happiness of the greatest number, Gandhi's philosophy is dedicated to ***Sarvodaya***. Hence, if the appliers of Gandhian philosophy bear this fact in mind at the time of actions, there is a great possibility of their success.

Thirdly, they should not become apprehensive of immediate result. They must become ready for a long-term fight. An action being carried out on the strength of non-violence can take a long time. Moreover, if directive principles set by the Mahatma himself, and later from time-to-time by other great Gandhians, are followed at the launch, and during the course of action, there remain all possibilities of success sooner or later. However, such an action will itself prove relevance, importance and adaptability of Gandhian philosophy for all-round development and peace.

References:

1. In which along with non-violent demonstrations, non-co-operation and boycott methods were adopted.

2. Especially through the means of boycott.

3. In protest women took the course of boycott of food stores particularly those of rice.

4. They also include: General Strike for suffrage in Sweden [1902

and 1909], Resistance to British Imposition of Conscription in Ireland [1917], A hunger strike by Marti in El Salvàdor [1930], Sit down and hunger strikes in Hungary [1934], the Peasants' agitation in Bolivia [1935], Massive Opposition to conscription and military instruction to force the Government to withdraw the law in New Zealand, Cocoa 'holdup' by farmers fighting against foreign export companies in Ghana [1937], a General strike in Nicaragua [1944], General Strike in connection with the 'Bogotá Revolt' in Columbia [1948], Occupation of haciendas by peasants syndicates in Bolivia [1952-3], General strike in Argentina [1959], Equal Rights Movement by Arabs in Israel [1960], ***Satyagraha*** campaign in Goa, India [1960], Students' revolt in El Salvador [1960], General strike in Ecuador [1961], Peasants' struggle in Brazil [1962-4], Grape workers' strike in Chile [1963], Peasants struggle in Peru [1963], Civilian insurrection in Vietnam [1963], Civilian insurrection in Sudan [1964-5], Demonstration in Northern Brazil involving Archbishop Dom Holder Camara [1966], Students' protests in Vietnam [1967-8], Protest in Londonderry in Northern Ireland [1968], Civilian insurrection lead by students and workers in France [1968], Mohawk campaign in New York, USA [1968], Students' strike and demonstration against regime in Brazil [1968], Students' demonstrations for university reform, Stanford in USA [1968], Fast unto death by Morarji Desai demanding restoration of democratic process in Gujarat Province in India [1975], Students' demonstrations in Mexico [1981], and the students' non-violent protests to pressurize administration to adopt codes guaranteeing living wages for workers manufacturing products in North Carolina, United States of America [1997-98].

5. Gandhi's arrival in South Africa in April 1893 was a coincident. A firm, 'Dada Abdullah & Co', had its extensive business in South Africa. One of its representatives in Rajkot [India]

approached Gandhi's elder brother to extend assistance in a civil suit involving UK Pounds 40, 000 pending in a South African Court. Although this firm already had a European lawyer but he too had to be helped by some one as the accounts and correspondence of the firm were in Gujarati. The engagement was for one year and remuneration, first class return fare and a sum of UK Pounds 105 all found. Gandhi closed with the offer and sailed for South Africa...

6. Particularly in Gujarat and U. P. under the able leadership of Sardar Vallabhbhai Patel and Pandit Jawaharlal Nehru respectively.

7. Started by breaking the Salt Law at Dandi in April 1930

8. According to Vinoba Bhave, a leading Gandhian thinker, ***"By peace or Shanti do not mean something static or perpetuation of the status quo. Shanti means something dynamic, something that develops the force of the individual, which develops the dynamic strength of the people to a degree that will enable to meet any situation."***

9. Welfare of all.

10. In his own words, ***"[This book by Ruskin] brought about an instant tenuous and practical transformation in my life."*** And, "... ***In Ruskin I have discovered some of my own firm beliefs and that is why I have taken with its message."***

11. 1819-1900

12. The new draft prepared by Mahatma Gandhi for the Indian National Congress was also named as his ***'Last Will and Testament'***. It became a historical document. Considering it to be important and significant I am including the whole text of the draft in appendix-2.

13. Popularly known as Acharya Vinoba Bhave [1895-1982], who was a close associate of the Mahatma, an educationist, a veteran freedom fighter, social reformer and thinker; he was selected as the first ***Satyagrahi*** on the eve of launching the Individual ***Satyagraha*** [1940] by Mahatma Gandhi himself. After Gandhi's passing away he took the task of reconstruction of India on Gandhian lines. Besides prestigious ***Ramon Magsaysay Award***, he was bestowed India's highest Civilian honour, the Bharat Ratna in 1983 for his unparalleled and outstanding services to the nation.

14. Donation of means of cultivation like wells, bullocks and other inputs from the rich for the poor donees of Bhoodan land.

15. Gift of labour or voluntary work.

16. Under the Gramdan scheme, eighty percent or more of villagers surrendered their ownership over land in the village-to-village committee for equitable distribution among them and the land so tendered did not come to less than fifty percent of the total land in the village. The re-division of land amongst them could be revised after early ten years period in accordance with their altered family needs. There was a great aim behind Gramdan plan of Vinoba Bhave as he saw Samyayoga, i.e. the Yoga of equality, similar to Sarvodaya of Mahatma Gandhi's conception, in it. In this regard he himself said, ***"After the attainment of Swarajya, we must aim at the establishment of Samyayoga, the Yoga of equality. We have named it Sarvodaya. You may call it by any name."***

17. Approximately fifty million acres of land.

18. Who after her active association with the ***'Chipko Movement'***, launched by renowned environmentalist Sunderlal Bahuguna with the purpose of saving trees in the hill areas of then Uttar

Pradesh, and now Uttrakhand, took initiative of starting the ***NAVDANYA***.

19. See reference 4 for the most of these organizations.

20. Murlidhar Devidas Amte [December 26, 1914 - February 9, 2008], popularly known as Baba Amte, was a respected social activist of India. He was the founder of several ***Ashrams*** for treatment and rehabilitation of leprosy patients, the disabled and other people from marginalized sections of society. ***Anandawana*** [Forest of Joy or Garden of Joy] in the remote and economically less privileged district of Chandrapur in Maharashtra province is the most well-known of such ***Ashrams*** where he himself stayed during his life. He also devoted his life to many other social causes, the most notable of which were environmental awareness, wildlife preservation and the ***Narmada Bachao Andolan***.

21. Founded by Bindeshwar Pathak [1943], an international renowned action socialist, reformer and expert of low-cost sanitation, biogas and rural development.

22. The GSS was established in 1957 at Vedachhi [Gujarat], which run a number of Gandhian Education Institutes [***Ashramshalas***] in which 4, 945 girls and boys from tribal areas are studying currently.

23. The VPSS, formed in 1952 at Vadod [Gujarat], which for the last one decade is working for spreading education in tribal areas, health in the rural areas and awakening among peasantry, particularly for preserving water.

24. Founded in 1968-69 in Gujarat, which for the last seven years is carrying our noteworthy activities relating to village development like roads construction, water management and distribution.

25. Established in 1967 at Vedachhi [Gujarat], which since 1990 is preparing Social workers committed to Gandhian ideas.

26. Formed fifty years ago in Mumbai, which besides educating people promotes Gandhian ideals all over India.

27. Made by Raju Hirani and produced by Vidhu Vinod Chopra.

28. In fact, it was during the first phase of the Civil Disobedience Movement [1930-31] when the word Gandhigiri was used for the first time by Sardar Vallabhbhai Patel in Mumbai, and the intention behind using this word by the Sardar was something else.

29. Indravadan Patel of Atali village.

Bibliography:

- Aiyar, PS, Stateless Indians in South Africa, KR Mehta, Allahabad [India], 1942
- Arillo, Cecilio, Breakaway: The Inside Story of the Four Day revolution in the Philippines, CTA and Associates, Manila [Philippines], 1986
- Bhave, Vinoba, Vinoba on Gandhi, Sarva Sewa Sangha, Pawnar, Wardha [India], 1973
- Evangelista, Susan, Non-Violence: A Text, ISP, Ateneo de Manila University [Philippines], 1994
- Gandhi, MK, An Autobiography or the Story of My Experiments with Truth, Navajivan, Ahmedabad [India], 1927
- Gandhi, MK, Constrictive Works: Meaning and Place, Navajivan Publishing House, Ahmedabad [India], 1948

- Gandhi, MK, Harijan Weekly, Published Under the Auspices of Harijan Sewak Sangh [1933-41]; by Navajivan Trust, Ahmedabad [India], Between 1942-48
- Gandhi, MK, India of My Dreams, Navajivan Publishing House, Ahmedabad [India], 1957 and Seventh Reprint 1999
- Gandhi, MK, Sarvodaya, Navajivan Publishing House, Ahmedabad, [India], 1955
- Gandhi, MK, Satyagraha in South Africa, Navajivan Publishing House, Ahmedabad [India], 1950
- Gandhi, MK, Young India Weekly [1919-31], Reprinted in 13 Volumes by Navajivan, Publishing House, Ahmedabad [India], 1984
- Fisher, Luis, Gandhi: His Life and Message for the World, New American Library [USA], 1991
- Hendricks, George, The Influence of Thoreau's Civil Disobedience on Gandhi's Satyagraha, The New England [Quarterly], December 1956
- Holmes, RL, Non-Violence in Theory and Practice, Wadsworth Publishing Company, California [USA], 1990
- Kumar, Ravindra [Edited], Global Peace: An International Journal of Philosophy, Peace, Education, Culture and Civilization...Volume 1-8, Number 1-4, Meerut [India], 2001-09
- Kumar, Ravindra, Non-Violence and its Philosophy, Dynamic Publications, Meerut [India], 2003
- Kumar, Ravindra, Theory and Practice of Gandhian Non-Violence, Mittal Publications, New Delhi [India], 2002

- Kumar, Ravindra, Towards Peace, Gyan Publishing House, New Delhi [India], 2007
- Shiva, Vandana, *Ecology and the Politics of Survival: Conflicts Over Natural Resources in India*, Sage Publications, Thousand Oaks, California [USA], 1991
- Shiva, Vandana, The Violence of the Green Revolution: Ecological degradation and political conflict in Punjab, Zed Press, New Delhi [India], 1992
- Tolstoy, Leo, The Law of Violence and The Law of Love, The Unicorn Press, London [UK], 1959

****

7

India: Democracy versus Mobocracy and Gandhi

"Democracy cannot be worked by twenty men sitting at the centre. For, it has to be worked from below by the people [consciously] from every village."

-MK Gandhi

Democracy in India

The roots of democracy in India are very deep. Probably it is India where democracy started functioning first. It is evident from the existence of institutions like ***Sabha***, ***Samiti*** and ***Viditha*** in the ***Vedic*** era.[1] Afterward, the existence of many republics[2] during the time of Gautama Buddha and Shakyamuni's advocacy in favour of democracy, his stress upon development of democratic institutions and noteworthy suggestions[3] made by him in this regard strengthens India's claim to it.

Generally, the democracy is recognized as a political institution. On the basis of it a political system of governance is conducted. But, in ancient times, the Buddhist assemblies in India have worked successfully in a democratic manner.[4] Hence, it has been more or less applied in religious sphere also. From this the significance and relevance of democracy for India can be well understood.

We can firmly believe that democracy is the best form of governance for a country like India. Along with political field there is a possibility of its functioning in economic and religious fields. We can assert this for the reason that India is a country of diversities and its unity is possible only by a democratic system of governance.

Democracy versus Mobocracy

Mahatma Gandhi, himself felt the importance and necessity of democracy for India, despite its being liable to be greatly abused.[5] That is why; he emphasized upon its constant development and maturity. Through this he wished transformation of his dream of ***Ramarajya*** into a reality. In the ***Ramarajya*** of his imagination each and everyone, weak or strong, gets equal opportunity to rise and his security and honour are guaranteed. In short, Gandhi's ***Ramarajya*** is an advanced form of democracy.

Now, the question arises, is there a possibility of transformation of Gandhi's dream of ***Ramarajya*** or an advanced form of democracy into a reality? If yes, then when? In this respect Mahatma Gandhi himself was not sure. Hence, he was not puzzled on these hypothetical questions. He knew that a human being always commits mistakes knowingly or unknowingly. He was also aware that one cannot get rid of them immediately and completely. Similarly, a manmade institution, it doesn't if it is a democracy, can also not become free of evils entirely and right away.

Therefore, Mahatma Gandhi, along with other necessities, particularly stressed upon discipline, equal respect of law by all and priority to social will over the individual will in a democracy. He was of the opinion that indiscipline, disrespect of law and priority to the individual will over the social will are among the main causes behind evils in a democracy. So, it is necessary to minimize them for making the democracy disciplined and enlightened.

Moreover, Mahatma Gandhi laid great emphasis on a healthy public opinion and expressed the need for responsible representation. The reason being if public opinion in democracy is not healthy and matured it can be converted into a mobocracy instead of giving strength to it. On many occasions and at different levels this can be observed in many countries of the world including India.

Similarly, if representatives in a democracy are not responsible, they weaken it instead of becoming its defenders. Sometimes it can also be experienced particularly in India. Therefore, Mahatma Gandhi called upon the people to reduce possibility of abuse in democracy to the minimum from time-to-time. He time and again emphasized upon making democratic system of governance firm, healthy, disciplined and responsible. Mahatma Gandhi's call to save democracy from becoming a mobocracy and to make it people-friendly and finally transforming it into a ***Swarajya*** was, and is, worth giving a thought.

Despite the large number of people coming together mobocracy can never be the reflection of a democracy. Due to lack of discipline and control over the crowd a mobocracy cannot transmit the will of the people. Hence, a mobocracy sometimes becomes more dangerous than a dictatorship. That is why; Mahatma Gandhi also said, ***"They [who are in a mob] have no mind, no premeditation. They act in frenzy."***[6]

How can a democracy be devoid of mobocracy? How can it be transformed into a real people's rule? How can it become a ***Swarajya***? Mahatma Gandhi was of the opinion that it was possible through the process of constant reforms in democracy and not in avoidance of it and that too in accordance with demand of time and prevailing circumstances. Simultaneously, for the rise of the institution of democracy he rightly called upon the people to carry on their duties and to maintain discipline.

In this process he further spoke about people's awareness: it meant people's consciousness of their duties, rights and responsibilities towards the nation. For, he fixed the responsibility of people's representatives on the one hand and the government on the other. He opposed the idea of such a democracy in which a handful of representatives, it doesn't matter if they are elected for a fixed period by the people itself, sat at the centre to work for it. Through that the real aim of democracy can never be achieved; the system cannot become a self-rule. In the words of Mahatma Gandhi himself:

> ***"Democracy cannot be worked by twenty men sitting at the centre. For, it has to be worked from below by the people [consciously] from every village."***[7]

Conclusion

Undoubtedly, Gandhi's stress upon an alert democracy is vital and significant. We should see no reason for an institution of democracy becoming unhealthy if its holders are disciplined and responsible. If citizens are conscious enough the democracy will definitely step forward towards a true self-rule. A disciplined, responsible and conscious democracy can become a true government of the people. Such a rule can turn into a ***Swarajya*** and can pave the way towards the ***Ramarajya*** of Mahatma Gandhi's imagination.

Hence, Gandhi's views regarding a democracy cannot be taken lightly. They must be analyzed minutely. An open debate on the vitality and relevance of them in the current perspectives should be organized. If they seem relevant as per the demand of time, they should be examined and adopted.

Today the whole world is looking at ***Ahimsa***-based ideas of Mahatma Gandhi. Particularly, institutions of higher learning are making critical analysis of his views on democracy. In such a situation the relevance, significance and utility of his ideas for India can be understood thoroughly.

References:

1. Approximately between 2000 and 1500 B. C.

2. Like the ***Shakya*** Republic, the ***Koliya*** Republic or the Vaishali Republic.

3. Besides his advocacy for a democracy, his commitment to this system can be seen from his advice to Licchavis of Vaishali to arrive at collective decisions and thereafter to take measures to implement them in cooperation of all.

4. Gandhi and Gandhism, pp 24-5

5. It is because democracy is a manmade institution and according to Mahatma Gandhi no manmade institution is free from evil or dangers. Rather, ***"the greater the institution the greater the chance of abuse...Democracy is a great institution and therefore it is liable to be greatly abused..."***

6. Young India, 8 September, 1920

7. Harijan, 18 January, 1948

Bibliography:

- Gandhi, MK, An Autobiography or the Story of My Experiments with Truth, Navajivan, Ahmedabad [India], 1927
- Gandhi, MK, Harijan Weekly, Published Under the Auspices of Harijan Sewak Sangh [1933-41]; by Navajivan Trust, Ahmedabad [India], Between 1942-48
- Gandhi, MK, Young India Weekly [1919-31], Reprinted in 13 Volumes by Navajivan, Publishing House, Ahmedabad [India],

1984

- Kumar, Ravindra, Gandhi and Gandhism, Part-1, World Peace Movement Trust, Meerut [India], 2001

****

Appendices

"It is my firm opinion that no culture has treasurers as rich as ours has. We have not known it, we have been made even to deprecate its study and depreciate its value."

-MK Gandhi

1

Cultural Heritage of India

"Nothing can be further from my thought than that we should become exclusive or erect barriers. But I do respectfully contend that an appreciation of other cultures can fully follow, never precede, an appreciation and assimilation of our own. It is my firm opinion that no culture has treasurers as rich as ours has. We have not known it, we have been made even to deprecate its study and depreciate its value. We have almost ceased to live it. An academic grasp without practice behind it is like an embalmed corpse, perhaps lovely to look at but nothing to inspire or ennoble. My religion forbids me to belittle or disregard other cultures, as it insists under pain of civil suicide upon imbibing and living my own"

[Source: Young India, Volume-3, Number-35, September 1, 1921]

2

Last Will and Testament of Mahatma Gandhi

"Though split into two, India having attained

political independence through means provided by the Indian National Congress, the Congress in its present shape and form, i.e., as a propaganda vehicle and parliamentary machine, has outlived its use. India has still to attain social, moral and economic independence in terms of its seven hundred thousand villages as distinguished from its cities and towns. The struggle for the ascendancy of civil over military power is bound to take place in India's progress towards its democratic goal. It must be kept out of unhealthy competition with political parties and communal bodies. For these and other similar reasons, the I. A. C. C. resolves to disband the existing Congress organization and flower into a ***Lok Sewak Sangh*** under the following rules with power to alter them as occasion may demand.

"Every ***Panchayat*** of five adult men or women being villagers or village-minded shall form a unit.

"Two such contiguous ***Panchayats*** shall form a working party under a leader elected from among them.

"When there are one hundred such ***Panchayats***, the fifty first grade leaders shall elect from among themselves a second leader and so on, the first grade leaders meanwhile working under the second grade leader. Parallel groups of two hundred ***Panchayats*** shall continue to be formed till they cover the whole of India, each succeeding group of ***Panchayats*** electing second grade leader after the manner of the first. All second grade leaders shall serve jointly for the whole of India and severally for their respective areas. The second grade leaders may elect, whenever they deem necessary, from among themselves a chief who will, during pleasure, regulate and command all the groups.

["As the final formation of provinces or districts is still in a state of flux, no attempt has been made to divide this group of servants into Provincial or District Councils and jurisdiction over the whole of India has been vested in the group or groups that may have been formed at any given time. It should be noted that this body of servants derive their authority or power from service ungrudgingly or wisely done to their master, the whole of India.]

1. Every worker shall be habitual wearer of ***Khadi*** made from self-spun or certified by the A. I. S. A. and must be a teetotaler. If a Hindu, he must have abjured untouchability in any shape or form in his own person or in his family and must be a believer in the ideal of inter-communal unity, equal respect for all religions and equality of opportunity and status for all irrespective of race, creed or sex;

2. He shall come in personal contact with every villager within his jurisdiction;

3. He shall enroll and train workers from amongst the

villagers and shall keep a register of all these;

4. He shall keep a record of his work from day-to-day;

5. He shall organize the villages so as to make them self-contained and self-supporting through their agriculture and handicrafts;

6. He shall educate the village folk in sanitation and hygiene and take all measures for prevention of ill health and disease among them;

7. He shall organize the education of the village folk from birth to death along the lines of ***Nai Talim***, in accordance with the policy laid down by the ***Hindustani Talimi Sangh***;

8. He shall see that those whose names are missing on the statutory voters' roll are duly entered therein;

9. He shall encourage those who have not yet acquired the legal qualification, to acquire it for getting the right of franchise; and

10. For the above purposes and other to be added from time-to-time, he shall train and fit himself in accordance with the rules laid down by the ***Sangh*** for the due performance of duty.

"The ***Sangh*** shall affiliate the following autonomous bodies:

1. A. I. S. A.;
2. A. I. V. I. A.;
3. ***Hindustani Talimi Sangh***;
4. ***Harijan Sewak Sangh***; and
5. ***Goseva Sangh***

Finance

"The Sangh shall raise finances for the fulfillment of its mission from among the villagers and others, special stress being laid on the collection of poor man's pice."

[Source: Mahatma: The Last Phase, Volume-2]

****

Who's Who

Einstein, Albert : [1879-1955] was an extraordinary professor at Zurich in 1909; became director of the Kaiser Wilhelm Physical Institute and professor in the University of Berlin in 1914; was appointed professor of Theoretical Physics at Princeton; emerged as a leading figure of the World Government Movement after the Second World War in 1945.

Facchini, Fiorenzo : An internationally renowned professor of Anthropology in the University of Bologna between 1978 and 2005; was responsible of the unit of Anthropology in the department of Evolutionistic and Experimental Biology and of the Museum of Anthropology in the same University; currently an emeritus professor in the University of Bologna; member of many scientific societies viz. the Academy of Sciences of Bologna, the Italian Institute of Anthropology, the Academy of Natural Sciences of Kazakhstan, and the New York Academy of Sciences.

Newton, Isaac : [1642-1727], was a great mathematician, physicist and one of the foremost scientists; earned reputation as a most highly esteemed natural philosopher of Europe for his theory of gravitation; joined the University of Cambridge in 1661; was elected a fellow of Trinity College in 1667; became Lucasian Professor of Mathematics in 1669.

Rolland, Romain : [1866-1944] was a renowned French writer, who won the Nobel Prize for Literature in 1915; his work Conversations with Rabindranath Tagore and Mohandas Karamchand Gandhi became famous after the Second World War as it revealed his concern for peace.

Ruskin, John : [1819–1900] was a British social thinker, a leading poet, an author and artist; his art and architecture-related essays were tremendously significant and influential in the Victorian and Edwardian eras.

Saraswati, Dayananda : [1824 -1883] was a great Vedic-Hindu scholar and the founder of the Arya Samaj [Society of Nobles] in 1875, and a believer in the infallible authority of the ***Vedas***; a leading Hindu social reformer who was the first Indian who gave the call for ***Swarajya*** in 1876, which was later furthered by Lokamanya Bal Gangadhar Tilak; was a supporter of equal rights of women; Swami Dayananda's immense contribution is his translation of the ***Vedas*** from ***Sanskrit*** into Hindi for the common man.

Tolstoy, Leo : [1828-1910] also known as **Lev Nikolayevich Tolstoy,** was a Russian writer widely regarded as among the greatest of European novelists; was the author of ***War and Peace, Anna Karenina, and The Kingdom of God Is Within You***; left a profound impact on people like Mahatma Gandhi and Martin Luther King, Jr.

Wellington, Duke of, or Wellesley, Arthur : [1769-1852] was an Anglo-Irish general, statesman and the victor of the Battle of Waterloo; was appointed Chief Secretary for Ireland in 1801; became the Prime Minister of Britain twice.

Zoroaster, Spitama : also known as **Zarathushtra** or **Zartosht**, was an ancient Iranian prophet and religious poet and the founder of Zoroastrianism.

****

Glossary of Indian Terms

Dharma	: Behaviour; deeds; duty; feeling; religious injunction
Goseva	: Serving the cows
Guru	: A spiritual guide; mentor; teacher; venerable
Harijan	: A devotee or servant of God; one belonging to Scheduled Caste; a weekly started by Mahatma Gandhi early in the fourth decade of twentieth century.
Hindustani	: Indian; of India
Jagatguru	: A widely revered teacher; world's mentor; a title of Vishnu, one of the supreme triple deities [the gods Brahma Vishnu and Shiva] and who is regarded as the preserver of the world during each period of its existence by Hindus
Jnana	: Knowledge
Khadi	: Handspun hand-woven cloth
Nai	: New

Panchayat	: A village council consisting of five, or more; a village court or arbitrating body
Parmodharmah	: Religion in grandeur
Rishi	: A sage; most learned; great scholar
Samskaras	: Instinct
Sangh/Sangha	: A society; group; association; body; federation; union; community
Sewak	: A Servant
Swarajya	: Self rule; own rule
Swami/Swamy	: An owner; proprietor; master; lord; king; a title of the Supreme Being
Talim	: Education
Talimi	: Concerning education; educational
Vedas	: The sacred early Hindu scriptures, four in number

****

Index

Q

R

S

****